D1002065

Should We Live Forever?

Should We

Live Forever?

The Ethical Ambiguities of Aging

GILBERT MEILAENDER

William B. Eerdmans Publishing Company
Grand Rapids, Michigan / Cambridge, U.K.

Published 2013 by
WM. B. EERDMANS PUBLISHING CO.
2140 Oak Industrial Drive N.E., Grand Rapids, Michigan 49505 /
P.O. Box 163, Cambridge CB3 9PU U.K.
www.eerdmans.com

Printed in the United States of America

17   16   15   14   13   7   6   5   4   3   2   1

Library of Congress Cataloging-in-Publication Data

Meilaender, Gilbert, 1946-
  Should we live forever : the ethical ambiguities of aging /
Gilbert Meilaender.
       p.   cm
  Includes bibliographical references and index.
  ISBN 978-0-8028-6869-5 (pbk. : alk. paper)
    1. Aging — Religious aspects — Christianity. 2. Aging — Moral and ethical
aspects. 3. Death — Moral and ethical aspects. 4. Older Christians — Religious
life. 5. Gerontology — Moral and ethical aspects.
I. Title.

  BV4580.M45 2013
  248.8'5 — dc23

"What the Bird Said Early in the Year" from *Poems* by C. S. Lewis. Copyright
© 1964 by the Executors of the Estate of C. S. Lewis and renewed 1992 by C. S.
Lewis Pte. Ltd. Reprinted by permission of Houghton Mifflin Harcourt Publishing Company. All rights reserved. Reprinted by permission of the C. S. Lewis
Company Ltd.

"An Ancient Story" by John Hall Wheelock, first published in the *Sewanee Review,*
vol. 81, no. 1, Winter 1973. Copyright 1973 by the University of the South. Reprinted with the permission of the editor.

Excerpts from "Night Thoughts in Age" and "Song on Reaching Seventy" by John
Hall Wheelock. Reprinted with the permission of Scribner, a Division of Simon &
Schuster, Inc., from *This Blessed Earth* by John Hall Wheelock. Copyright © 1973,
1974, 1975, 1976 by John Hall Wheelock. Copyright © 1978 by the estate of John
Hall Wheelock. All rights reserved.

To Nathanael and Flora
whose youth is both burden and blessing

Contents

Introduction

Science continues to be a channel for magic — the belief that for the human will, empowered by knowledge, nothing is impossible.

John Gray, *The Immortalization Commission*

Do not cast me off in the time of old age;
forsake me not when my strength is spent. . . .
till I proclaim thy might
to all the generations to come.

Psalm 71:9, 18b

A FEW YEARS ago I was fortunate enough to receive a grant from the University of Chicago's New Science of Virtues Project, funded by the John Templeton Foundation. The focus of my project was to be virtue (and virtues) in relation to anti-aging research; and, at least initially, I believe I was thinking in terms of a rather standard bioethical exploration of ongoing research into age-retardation and extension of the life span. It was not long, though, before it became apparent to me that the project could not be done in a metaphysically neutral way. Inevitably, religious beliefs kept creeping in. I have not so much tried to defend those beliefs as to explore their significance for human aging and attempts to retard it. That we often desire, even greedily desire, longer life is clear; whether what we desire is truly desirable is harder to say.

The classical understanding of virtue referred to what philosophers in recent decades have come to call human flourishing — the excellence that realizes and expresses the full potential of our human nature. Because that nature is an embodied one, we might suppose that, whatever human flourishing involves, it must include the aging and decline that characterize bodily organisms. Since, however, we are *rational* animals, our full potential may be realized only through our freedom to remake ourselves, transcending indefinitely the limits of the body. We try — rightly, I think — to cure and even eradicate disease, but whether we should approach aging in the same way is deeply puzzling. Still more, when we notice that some of the more ambitious proposals for age-retardation seem rather like a desire to escape bodily existence itself, we may begin to wonder whether the aim is to transcend or to transgress the body's limits.

Moreover, if we are not only rational but also *ecstatic* animals (whose self is, as Søren Kierkegaard put it, a relation of temporal and eternal), there can be no human flourishing that is isolated from our relation to God. Prolongation of this life, however long, could not really satisfy the thirst that we experience. Still, no one should suppose that religious belief eliminates whatever is puzzling about the project of life-extension. In fact, it may in some ways complicate our struggle to gain clarity. Thus, George Weigel recounts Cardinal Francis George having asked a few years ago, with a vivid sense of the question's paradoxical strangeness: "Do you realize that we're going to spend the rest of our lives trying to convince people that suffering and death are good for you?"[1] If this life is God's good gift, more of it seems like a good thing; yet the thirst for more may easily become not the way that leads to God but an end in itself.

The first three chapters that follow attempt to think, from several different angles, about whether more life, indefinitely more life, is a goal we ought to pursue. In the first chapter I survey some of what we know about aging and age-retardation, in order to suggest that science cannot itself tell us what our aims should be. And I note — though not, I hope, without recognizing the worth of more life — what would be lost if a substantial increase in the maximum human life span turned old age into "a kind of endless middle age" and drastically altered the relation between the generations.[2]

---

1. George Weigel, *Letters to a Young Catholic* (New York: Basic Books, 2004), p. 180.

2. Daniel Callahan, "Why We Must Set Limits," in *A Good Old Age? The Paradox of Setting Limits,* ed. Paul Homer and Martha Holstein (New York: Simon & Schuster, 1990), p. 26.

In the second chapter I consider some of the most far-reaching, perhaps in some cases bizarre, proposals to extend life by detaching it from its organic base. Whether this is simply transcending the givens of our current existence or transgressing the limits that should characterize our humanity is, of course, a fundamental question. Confidence in historical progress is not the same as Christian hope. Only to the degree that we find ways to honor the body and to understand ourselves as "on the way" to a flourishing not of our own making can the virtue of hope really shape our being and doing.

In the third chapter I suggest that no approach to the question of life-extension and age-retardation will be free of normative commitments. Indeed, the palpable thirst for an indefinitely extended life, for an escape from mystery and contingency, animates the project of life-prolongation more than moderns might wish to admit. Observing that "science and the occult have interacted at many points," the philosopher John Gray writes that, in the struggle for a kind of humanly produced immortality, "the hope of life after death has been replaced by the faith that death can be defeated."[3] Yet, in our world that thirsts for longer life there is, nonetheless, a substantial body of literature arguing that immortality, whether of our own making or of God's, would be undesirable. To examine it is to see that there is no single or neutral understanding of immortality.

It is also important to reflect upon the project of indefinite life-extension from the perspective not simply of virtue (in the singular) but of particular virtues. The virtues are not just means to an end; they are elements of a life well lived. In the fourth, fifth, and sixth chapters I examine three aspects of a virtuous life in relation to the project of indefinite life-extension. There are no perfect terms to mark out these elements of a life well lived. But in pondering the relation between the generations and the ways

3. John Gray, *The Immortalization Commission: Science and the Strange Quest to Cheat Death* (New York: Farrar, Straus and Giroux, 2011), pp. 6, 207-8.

in which successful programs of age-retardation might alter those relations, I speak of *generativity.* In thinking about the temporal character of life as we know it, I reflect upon *patience;* for, after all, "only the old . . . can know what it means to go from past through present to future."[4] And in order to think about life's stages, I ask whether a *complete* life, a life that is integral and whole, is possible or desirable for us.

I cannot promise readers that these six chapters will provide a straightforward path to clear answers about how we ought to think about aging and the scientific (but also quasi-religious) project of age-retardation. Indeed, I have seldom thought or written about a subject that I find more puzzling. Temperamentally disposed as I am to think that a virtuous life must acknowledge the goodness even of decline and old age, I am also deeply drawn to the words of the poet John Hall Wheelock, which I quote in the first chapter: "More time — oh, but a little more."

In a less refined and perhaps non-philosophical way, sports fans are accustomed to thinking about this puzzle, and examples of it arise frequently. In November of 2011 the stunning news of allegations of sexual abuse connected to the Penn State football program was the topic of endless conversations. Those revelations brought an end to the long and storied career of eighty-four-year-old Penn State football coach Joe Paterno. Many defended him vigorously. But others of us were inclined to think he might have stubbornly held on too long, unwilling to accept the waning of his abilities and influence. Brett Favre's seeming inability to retire generated similar discussion and disagreement for several years.

Was it sad, as I am inclined to think, to watch the great Willie Mays play out the string at the end of his career, when he was no longer even a shadow of the Mays whose great catch in the 1954 World Series I once watched? Or was it, as others are eager to argue, just fine that he should continue to play as long as some team would

4. Daniel Callahan, *Setting Limits: Medical Goals in an Aging Society* (New York: Simon and Schuster, 1987), p. 43.

give him the opportunity? There is, I suppose, no right answer to that question — hence, the puzzles of my topic. But I at least will always prefer the way Ted Williams's career ended — with a majestic home run in his last at-bat, immortalized (!) in John Updike's famous essay, "Hub Fans Bid Kid Adieu."[5]

It was once common for Christians to pray words such as the following: "Grant . . . that, as the end of my earthly life draws ever nearer, I may not grow to be a part of these fleeting earthly surroundings, but rather grow more and more conformed to the life of the world to come."[6] I am not certain we can evaluate the scientific project of indefinite life-extension properly, neither denying the great goodness of life nor being enslaved to the thirst to live, unless the words of that prayer make some sense to us.

Accepting decline and preparing to relinquish the quite understandable desire for "more life" does not mean turning against the goodness of life. "Do not cast me off in the time of old age," the psalmist prays, so that I can tell the story of your might to generations yet to come. The gift is not simply set aside or disdained; it is handed on, affirmed, and honored. In that way we acknowledge our responsibilities and affirm the relation between the generations to the very end of our lives.

It remains only to express my gratitude for the grant from the Science of Virtues Project (and duly to note that the opinions I express in these essays do not necessarily reflect the views of the John Templeton Foundation); to thank the other participants in that project, with whom and from whom I learned much along the way; to thank the Notre Dame Center for Ethics and Culture (and David Solomon, who was then its director) for the opportunity to be the Center's Remick Fellow in the 2010-11 academic year; to thank Jenny Hoffman for her editorial labor and (even more) her persistence in getting reprint per-

5. First published in the *New Yorker,* the piece has been often anthologized. See John Updike, "Hub Fans Bid Kid Adieu," in *Baseball: A Literary Anthology,* ed. Nicholas Dawidoff (New York: The Library of America, 2002), pp. 301-17.

6. John Baillie, *A Diary of Private Prayer* (New York: Charles Scribner's Sons, 1949), p. 129.

missions; and to note the happy accident (if there are any accidents) that this project provided the occasion for my discovery of the poetry of John Hall Wheelock, who wrote the fitting words quoted later in this book: "Age is the hour for praise."

CHAPTER ONE

How Shall We Think about Aging?

The anti-aging medicine of the not-so-distant future would treat what we have usually thought of as the whole, the healthy, human life as a condition to be healed.

The President's Council on Bioethics, *Beyond Therapy*

The highest expression of human dignity and human nature is to try to overcome the limitations imposed on us by our genes, our evolution, and our environment.

Ronald Bailey, *Liberation Biology*

An earlier version of this chapter appeared as "Thinking about Aging," in *First Things* 212 (April 2011): 37-43.

AS THE NUMBER of our years increases, as we age in that simple chronological sense, we also age in a more important and profound sense. Gradually but progressively our bodies begin to function less effectively, and that increasing loss of function makes us more vulnerable to disease and death. Nevertheless, we should distinguish aging from disease. Unlike disease, aging is a normal stage of life that seems "built in." It makes us more vulnerable to disease but is not itself pathology. No one dies because his hair turns gray, and the diseases often associated with old age can occur even apart from aging. Hence, to say that someone died "from old age" simply means, as biologist Tom Kirkwood puts it, that his hold on life had "become so precarious that, had it not been this particular cause of death today, it would have been another tomorrow."[1]

Aging might be said to be natural for human beings in the sense that it happens to all of us (unless, of course, we die before getting a chance to age). And while few people seem to relish growing old, even fewer want to die young, without the opportunity to age. Nor is aging natural only for human beings. All mammals age, and with only rare possible exceptions (such as the sea anemone), so do all living organisms (though in the wild most of them die too soon to age). We grow, we experience puberty, we mature — and we age. That is the course of a healthy human life. If we do not think of the other, earlier stages of our development as problems to be overcome, and if aging itself is not a disease, then why think of it as a problem that needs solving?

One reason we hesitate to adopt such a benign view of aging is, of course, that it seems so inextricably connected to death. Thus, Lewis Thomas, imagining in one of his elegant essays that ours might someday be a species free of disease, is quite naturally driven to ask: How then will we die? And, by way of answer, he tries to picture how we might simply wear out without breaking down in

1. Tom Kirkwood, *Time of Our Lives: The Science of Human Aging* (Oxford and New York: Oxford University Press, 1999), p. 22.

any particular way — without, that is, falling prey to any disease. Aging then becomes "an orderly, drying up process, terminated by the most natural of events."[2]

The moral would seem to be: Aim to cure or ameliorate the diseases associated with old age but accept aging itself. Aim not at more years but at better, healthier years. To be sure, better health will probably mean a somewhat longer average life span, but it will not necessarily alter the maximum life span for human beings. The result will be platitudinous: adding life to years, not necessarily years to life.

Sensible as this seems in many ways, it may not "make sense." If it is good to extend life by curing illness and relieving infirmity — knocking off age-associated diseases one by one in a way almost everyone seems to approve — why not also try to slow the aging process itself and extend life still further? Moreover, if we want to preserve health and overcome specific diseases, one way to do it would be to retard the process of aging, which is closely tied to increased vulnerability to illness. Indeed, doing that (were we really able) might be a more effective way of enhancing health than simply overcoming diseases one at a time.

Thus, even if aging — unlike disease — is natural, a part of "the whole, the healthy, human life," as the President's Council on Bioethics put it,[3] as long as we cannot say the same of disease we may find it hard to argue against work that retards aging and (in so doing) extends the maximum life span. Though theoretically separate, disease and aging are inextricably intertwined in our lives. We seem driven — sometimes, at least, for the best of reasons — to try to overcome even the limit of years imposed on us "by our genes, our evolution, and our environment."[4] Whether doing so is, as Ronald Bailey puts it, the highest expression of our

2. Lewis Thomas, "The Deacon's Masterpiece," in *The Medusa and the Snail: Notes of a Biology Watcher* (New York: Viking Press, 1979), p. 136.

3. The President's Council on Bioethics, *Beyond Therapy: Biotechnology and the Pursuit of Happiness* (New York: Regan Books, 2003), p. 201.

4. Ronald Bailey, *Liberation Biology* (Amherst, NY: Prometheus Books, 2005), p. 61.

dignity, I doubt. But it is not easy to argue that we should entirely forego the attempt.

⌗   ⌗   ⌗

From the start, we need to think about how to think about growing old — and, in particular, how to think not simply of aging but of *human* aging. This will require that we learn from but also move beyond what has become the standard way to think about aging. Scholars study both *why* we age and *how* we age. The first seems to invite talk about a purpose, the second about a mechanism. The first is more germane to my inquiry here.

Why do we age? The dominant answer today is that of evolutionary biology, which goes something like this: We age because nature has relatively little stake in keeping us alive beyond our reproductive years. Insofar as we may speak of our lives having a point, it is to be carriers of DNA. Having passed that on to the next generation, we are dispensable. Any genetic trait harmful enough to cause death before the reproductive years will have difficulty surviving the filter of natural selection. Those who have such traits are less likely to reproduce, less likely to be effective carriers and transmitters of DNA. And, by contrast, natural selection will have relatively little effect upon harmful genes if those harms appear only later in life in the post-reproductive years.

Of course, we may continue to hang around for a while after we have produced the next generation, but as we do we inevitably suffer from genes whose harmful effects manifest themselves only in those later years. Natural selection having less need to eliminate them, they accumulate and start to take a toll on us. We begin to experience the effects of a gradual and generalized physical deterioration. Because nature's interest in us all along has been simply an interest in reproduction, in the transmitting of our genes, it has paid relatively less attention to maintaining us beyond the years crucial for that task. Focusing on reproduction rather than maintenance, nature has not bothered to weed out changes that make us more vulnerable to disease and death: a weakening immune system, increasingly brittle bones, a clogged cardiovascular system, deteriorating sensory systems. These are part of the natural process of aging; but, of course, they are also closely linked to a wide range of diseases — pneumonia, fractures, heart disease, hearing and vision loss.

Tom Kirkwood has labeled this account of why we age the "disposable soma" theory.[5] The idea is that, from the point of view of genes trying to transmit their DNA to the next generation, the body is little more than a carrier and is not made to survive indefinitely. It will eventually die anyway, so not a lot should be invested in sustaining it beyond that reproductive task. "Disposable soma" is a label worth pondering. It may sound mechanistic, but it is pervasively marked by metaphors drawn from human experience. For example, it is human beings, not genes, who have a point of view. It is not genes but living organisms that have purposes and goals. It is human beings, not genes, who care about a "next generation." And if the body seems from the perspective of this theory to be disposable, we should remember what body is being so characterized. It is *our* body — which is the place of our personal presence, through which we are linked to our world and to others, apart from which we can scarcely imagine our own continuing identity. "Before I was conceived there was no me," philosopher Christine Overall writes, "and no possibility of being a me. Some philosophers have claimed that my genetic material might have come into being earlier than it did. But even if this is empirically possible, the me that exists now is the product of the whole complex of experiences that have occurred since my birth or even since my conception."[6] Hence, whatever the usefulness of the disposable soma theory — and no doubt it is useful for many purposes — we may wonder whether it is well suited to help us think about how long it is good for us to live.

---

5. Kirkwood, *Time of Our Lives*, p. 65.
6. Christine Overall, *Aging, Death, and Human Longevity: A Philosophical Inquiry* (Berkeley: University of California Press, 2003), p. 27.

It is also instructive to underscore the close connection this standard explanation discerns between aging and reproduction. "The rule, simply stated," as John Medina puts it, "is this: If you have sex, you will eventually die."[7] From the perspective of the well-being of our species, there is little reason to devote the body's energies to tasks of cell repair and maintenance aimed at sustaining any of us into an old age that extends well beyond our reproductive years. A favorite example of evolutionary biologists is the contrast between semelparous species (which reproduce only once) and iteoparous species (which may reproduce repeatedly). Semelparous organisms generally die after reproducing and, therefore, will not be around to provide care for their offspring. (They usually produce a large number of offspring, which compensates for the fact that they will not live to provide care.) If, however, they are prevented from reproducing, they will live much longer than their normal life span. Thus, science itself invites us to think about the intertwining of reproduction with length of life and the relation between the generations.

The same lesson can be drawn from studies of caloric restriction in rodents (and, more recently, in rhesus monkeys). Indeed, a rather drastic reduction in calories seems to be the one certain method for retarding the aging process, even if we cannot say for certain how it works. Since the mid-1930s researchers have known that dietary restriction extends life. A diet containing normal healthy ingredients but with 30-40 percent fewer calories than usual has been shown to extend the life span of some mice and rats well beyond that of others whose food intake has not been so restricted. The standard explanation seems reasonable: If food is scarce, the body's energy resources focus on cell maintenance rather than reproduction, increasing the animal's chances of surviving longer and making time for the animal to reproduce when food becomes more readily available. Delaying reproduction extends the period of life when natural selection is effective. But, of course, a price is paid: Caloric restriction is closely

7. John J. Medina, *The Clock of Ages: Why We Age — How We Age — Winding Back the Clock* (Cambridge: Cambridge University Press, 1996), p. 20.

tied to delayed puberty and reduced fertility. Moreover, it is not impossible that we might one day be able to manipulate the genome in ways that regulate reproduction *in order to* extend youthfulness and retard aging. At any rate, however we account for the connection, it indicates that aging affects not only individuals or a single generation; it has implications for the relation *between* the generations.

If, then, we take the standard account of why we age and try to derive moral advice from it, one's first thought might be: Don't have children, and I'll live longer. But that would be to misunderstand, for nature is focused not on our well-being but on that of our genes. So, instead, the moral advice that might seem to follow is: Have children, the more the better, the sooner the better. In that way we can be effective transmitters of our DNA and take our place in nature's larger and grander undertaking. If this happens to make life burdensome for us, we can take comfort in knowing that we have played our part well. Indeed, anything — including living well into old age — that makes us less likely or less eager to have children seems contrary to nature's ongoing project. "From an evolutionary point of view, the name of the game is," as Robert Arking puts it, "to play again (i.e., the whole point of being a reproductive adult is to pass copies of your genes on to the next generation)."[8]

We are disinclined to draw such moral lessons from the account evolutionary biologists give of why we age — and with good reason. That account may be able to tell us about *changes* that have occurred during our natural history, but it cannot tell us whether these are *improvements*. The fact that we can and do appeal to "nature" to support quite different versions of moral advice should, as Stephen Jay Gould once wrote, "teach us two lessons: first, that we have a remarkable capacity for self-delusion in projecting our hopes and fears on nature and re-deriving them as 'fact,' and second, that

---

8. Robert Arking, "Extending Human Longevity: A Biological Probability," in *The Fountain of Youth: Cultural, Scientific, and Ethical Perspectives on a Biomedical Goal,* ed. Stephen G. Post and Robert H. Binstock (Oxford and New York: Oxford University Press, 2004), p. 181.

nature is sufficiently rich and multifarious to say yes (in part) to any human vision."[9]

In a remembrance of his friend and colleague C. S. Lewis, Nevill Coghill recounted a conversation that took place once when he and Lewis were dining with Rector Marett of Exeter College.

> Marett was a man of abundant geniality and intelligence, always ready with friendly freshets of conversation and new gambits of gossip to entertain a guest. Presently he turned to Lewis and said:
>
> "I saw in the papers this morning that there is some scientist-fellah in Vienna, called Voronoff — some name like that — who has invented a way of splicing the glands of young apes onto old gentlemen, thereby renewing their generative powers! Remarkable, isn't it?"
>
> Lewis thought.
>
> "I would say, 'unnatural.' "
>
> "Come, come! 'Unnatural'! What do you mean, *'unnatural'?* Voronoff is a part of Nature, isn't he? What happens in Nature must surely be natural? Speaking as a philosopher, don't you know" — (Marett taught Philosophy) — "I can attach no meaning to your objection; I don't understand you!"
>
> "I am sorry, rector; but I think any philosopher from Aristotle to — say — Jeremy Bentham, would have understood me."
>
> "Oh, well, we've got beyond Bentham by now, I hope. If Aristotle or he had known about Voronoff, they might have changed their ideas. Think of the possibilities he opens up! You'll be an old man yourself, one day."
>
> *"I would rather be an old man than a young monkey."*[10]

This anecdote, which refers, in fact, to a well-known episode in early attempts to develop anti-aging therapies, is not only amusing; it is also philosophically to the point.[11]

9. Stephen Jay Gould, "Biological Musings," *The New York Times Book Review* 84 (May 6, 1979): 33.

10. Nevill Coghill, "The Approach to English," in *Light on C. S. Lewis,* ed. Jocelyn Gibb (London: Geoffrey Bles, 1965), p. 61.

11. For an account of the Voronoff episode, see Arnold Kahn, "Regaining Lost Youth:

We cannot read ethical principles off the accounts given us by evolutionary biologists, because moral reasoning requires something more complicated. What we need, as Alasdair MacIntyre once put it, is not only a description of human nature in its "untutored" condition but also at least some sense of what it would mean for that nature to be fully realized. The principles that obligate us and the virtues that shape us provide the guidance and direction we need to move from our natural condition in that first (untutored) sense to our natural condition in the second (fulfilled and flourishing) sense.[12] This teleological conception of ethics — in which the imperative makes possible growth from the descriptive to the attractive — bears similarity to the physician's work of medical diagnosis. The physician begins not only with the patient's symptoms and illness but also with a conception of health toward which the patient needs to be helped and directed. And the physician's prescription mediates that movement toward health. When we think normatively about our nature, we cannot avoid something like this threefold scheme.

The account given by evolutionary biologists tells us what is "natural" only in the sense that it happens all around us, and that sense will give us little traction when normative questions are our concern. "We must," as the great nineteenth-century philosopher Henry Sidgwick once wrote, "give a special precision to the meaning of 'natural'; since in a sense . . . any impulse is natural, but it is manifestly idle to bid us to follow Nature in this sense."[13] Ethics would then become, as T. H. Huxley (Darwin's bulldog!) himself put it, merely "applied Natural History," in which theft and murder may be as natural as philanthropy.[14] But we are looking for something different, for the natural in

---

The Controversial and Colorful Beginnings of Hormone Replacement Therapy in Aging," *The Journals of Gerontology, Series A: Biological Sciences and Medical Sciences* 60A, no. 2 (February 2005): 142-47.

12. Alasdair MacIntyre, *After Virtue: A Study in Moral Theory* (Notre Dame, IN: University of Notre Dame Press, 1981), pp. 50-51.

13. Henry Sidgwick, *The Methods of Ethics,* 7th ed. (orig. ed. 1907; Indianapolis: Hackett Publishing Company, 1981), p. 81.

14. Thomas H. Huxley, "Evolution and Ethics," the Romanes Lecture, 1893, in *Evolution and Ethics and Other Essays* (New York: D. Appleton and Company, 1894), p. 73.

the sense of a completion or fulfillment of our inborn possibilities in ways that contribute to human well-being.

Although talking about "why" we age seems to invite us to think teleologically about the point or purpose of this natural process, the account given by evolutionary biology actually avoids all such talk of fulfillment and prescribes nothing. DNA has no aims or purposes, but we — who are not just collections of DNA — do. Hence, this account is insufficient as a guide to *human* aging. It cannot illumine what is natural for us in the distinctively moral sense: how we ought to live in order to flourish as human beings. What is natural for us in this sense is not what happens to us all the time but what is appropriate to beings of the sort we are. And, therefore, if we want to think about whether an indefinite prolongation of life is in accord with or contrary to our nature, we will need to reflect in ways that are normative from the outset. Rather than disposing of the soma, we will need to consider the goods to which our embodied human nature itself inclines.

⧗   ⧗   ⧗

Prolonging life might, of course, take several different forms or have several different meanings. All things, even inorganic materials that are not alive, get older in one sense as years pass. But they do not age in the way living organisms do. We could perhaps prolong the life of many inorganic objects by taking great care to preserve them, but it would make no sense to talk of retarding their aging process. For living organisms, however, it does make sense to think about both life-prolongation and age-retardation. They are closely connected, but not identical. Prolonging life for more years, getting older in that simple sense, is not quite the same as retarding aging.

If the upshot of anti-aging research were that more and more of us — like Jonathan Swift's Struldbrugs — lived in a condition of indefinitely prolonged aging or senescence, what Francis Fukuyama has called "the national nursing home scenario," few would regard that as a successful outcome.[15] Alas, that upshot is for us no longer entirely a matter for the subjunctive mood, as if it were still a condition contrary to fact. For many in our society it has already become the other side — the downside — of our remarkable medical progress.

But well before the marvels of modern medicine, our ancestors recognized the ambivalence of our thirst for longer life. The author of the sayings in Ecclesiastes — whoever precisely "Qoheleth" may have been — had no trouble picturing an old man dragging himself along like a grasshopper, taking no pleasure in his continuing days and years. No wonder Qoheleth famously said that there is "a time to be born, and a time to die" (Eccles. 12:1-8; 3:2).[16]

Equally powerful is the figure in Greek myth of Tithonus — a mortal man loved by Aurora, goddess of the Dawn. She asked Zeus to make Tithonus immortal but failed to ask in addition that he remain forever young. He became, therefore, an old man — unable to move, babbling endlessly, but unable to die. "I wither slowly in thine arms," he says in Tennyson's famous poem, and is driven finally to say "take back thy gift."[17] If such an indefinitely extended life were the fruit of anti-aging research, no doubt many would likewise pray, "take back thy gift." One of the dangers of this form of life-prolongation is, in fact, that it may tempt many not merely to utter such a prayer but — deciding that if we cannot live well we should not live at all — to reject the gift entirely. In any case, life-prolongation that is not also age-retardation is unlikely to offer what we really want.

If, therefore, our present circumstance — in which many people will experience prolonged and progressive senescence — is undesirable, and if it tempts us to love life less than we should, we do well to think about other conditions at which we might aim under

---

15. Francis Fukuyama, *Our Posthuman Future* (New York: Farrar, Straus and Giroux, 2002), p. 69.

16. Throughout, quotations from the Bible are taken from the Revised Standard Version.

17. Alfred, Lord Tennyson, "Tithonus," at www.readprint.com/work-1423/Tithonus-Lord-Alfred-Tennyson. Accessed November 1, 2011.

the rubrics of life-prolongation or age-retardation. Without taking as our goal any increase in the maximum life span possible for human beings, we might, for instance, aim at what is often called "compressed morbidity." The target here is primarily disease and, only indirectly, aging itself. The goal is that for (almost) as long as we live, we should live largely free of disease and disability. Then, it seems, after a (presumably) somewhat longer life than the current average life span, we would die — suddenly and rather quickly.

Something like this, it should be apparent, is what many in our society hope for. Live as long as we can at the peak of our powers — and then just fall off the cliff. We might idealize it less, however, if we thought about it more. If the idea is that we live, almost up till the end, a life that is vigorous and relatively free of disease or disability, why would we want it to end? The decline that aging involves is, in a way, a gradual and (at least sometimes) gentle preparation for the cliff toward which we move. Even now we are especially distressed when someone dies at or near the peak of his powers. If we all died that way, would that be an improvement?

Moreover, it is not clear — or, at least, not clear to me — that we can coherently think through the image of compressed morbidity. The idea is that we live a somewhat longer and (until the very end) disease-free life, and then we die suddenly. But we must ask: Die of what? That is not easy to say. The answer cannot simply be: of old age. To be old is merely to be increasingly vulnerable to a variety of diseases. If one or another of these is to relieve us quickly of this mortal coil, we will still have had to age. Bones must still have become brittle, sensory systems needed for vision and hearing must have deteriorated, our immune system must have weakened. (Must plaques and tangles have built up in the brain? But then we may have difficulty distinguishing this vision of life-prolongation from the first, prolonged senescence.) In short, the longer we think about compressed morbidity as an approach to age-retardation, the harder it is to picture clearly.

In any case, the thirst for anti-aging remedies is, I think, a desire for something more. It is a search for methods that — without entirely eliminating the aging process — slow its pace considerably and thereby extend even the maximum life span. Or, more far-reaching still, it is a desire for means that will continuously overcome the biological processes of aging by finding ways to reverse the kinds of change and loss that for now mark our post-reproductive years. The first of these aspirations — slowing the pace of aging — might leave intact a kind of life cycle, simply stretching it out over a more extended time period. The second, a more thoroughgoing continual rejuvenation, would not only extend the maximum life span but would do so in a way that no longer seemed to leave place for stages of life. Each, at any rate, has in mind an *indefinite* prolongation of life through retardation of aging.

⧗   ⧗   ⧗

Why not aggressively pursue such strategies for retarding aging?

Once we are clear that evolutionary biology, which discerns no point or purpose in natural processes, cannot answer this question, we are free to learn what we can from more modest, less far-reaching reflection on human nature. Normative thinking cannot, after all, proceed in complete isolation from what we think we know about the sort of creature we are. Human beings are characterized by tendencies, by desires, and by limits. If these provide no ready-made ethical principles, we must at least keep them in mind when we think about what it would mean for us to flourish. And even if we bracket entirely talk about cosmic purposes, we may be able to discern something about the natural ends of human life and what will or will not fulfill those ends. "Although," as Larry Arnhart puts it, "the evolutionary process does not serve goals, the organisms emerging from that process do."[18]

Moreover, as Arnhart notes, although evolutionary biology thinks

18. Larry Arnhart, *Darwinian Natural Right: The Biological Ethics of Human Nature* (Albany: State University of New York Press, 1998), p. 245.

in terms of a natural selection that has no purposes, in many other ways modern biology is shot through with such purposive language. For example, the ability of living organisms to maintain a stable body temperature and balance of bodily fluids — homeostasis — is a teleological concept. We examine not only *how* this takes place but also *why* — to what ends — the living body works to sustain this balance. Likewise, if we ask what the acorn is made for, the answer is in terms of a natural end: to develop into an oak tree. Or, put more fully, to fulfill its nature by developing into a thing appropriate to its kind. To be sure, we find ourselves less confident — and less in agreement — when we ask a question such as, For what is a human being made? But this is the sort of question that can begin to push us to think about the meaning of human aging. It is complicated, moreover, by the fact that human beings are made, among other things, to act with a freedom that regularly transcends and reshapes limits and structures that have seemed to be "givens" in human existence. That freedom, too, is part of our nature, and it requires that we be cautious when thinking about the meaning of human aging. This does not mean, however, that we are left entirely without insight.

Thus, for example, when Arnhart lists "twenty natural desires" that are, he says, "so deeply rooted in human nature that they will manifest themselves in some manner across history in every human society," first on his list is the desire for "a complete life."

> Human beings generally desire life. Like other animals, they pass through a life cycle from birth to maturity to death. Every human society is organized to manage the changing desires associated with this life cycle, which passes through distinct stages such as infancy, juvenility, adolescence, adulthood, and old age. . . . Although human beings will risk their lives for a good cause, they generally agree that to be fully happy one must live out one's natural life span.[19]

19. Arnhart, *Darwinian Natural Right*, pp. 244-45.

Two somewhat different claims are closely united here. Human beings desire life. And they desire a complete life (understood in terms of the full life cycle). These do not quite come to the same thing. An indefinitely extended life might not be a life still shaped by stages culminating in old age.

Among the twenty natural desires Arnhart thinks we can identify in human beings is the desire to give and receive parental care. Attending to it shows us at least part of what it means to have a "complete life." "Parent-child bonding is," Arnhart writes, "naturally good for human beings."[20] This way of rearing the next generation has characterized almost all human communities and has been remarkably difficult to eliminate even in small communities that have intentionally sought to do so. The parent-child bond as a way of rearing the next generation seems to conform better to our nature than other possible ways. Under very special circumstances (such as in the kibbutzim) it may be possible for a time to set aside this bond. Even then, however, as Arnhart notes, the evidence suggests that doing so is generally experienced as a considerable sacrifice.

Once we begin to attend to the parent-child bond, or more generally to the relation between generations, we have begun to think not just of life but of a "complete life" — a life marked in some way by stages and movement, a life that has shape and not just duration, a life whose moments are not identical but take their specific character from their place in the whole. Moreover, it is difficult to imagine a "relation between the generations" that does not include aging — coming into being and going out of being. This may stand in some tension with the thirst for indefinitely more life that most of us sometimes experience, but it is hard to imagine a characteristically human life without it. And from this perspective, a simple thirst for more (and more) life might seem to carry an unmistakable whiff of narcissism, for it is hard to imagine how we can act responsibly toward the generations that succeed us if we cling firmly (and desper-

20. Arnhart, *Darwinian Natural Right*, p. 29.

ately?) to our own continued youthfulness. Doing that would cause us to lose the shape that gives wholeness and integrity to our lives.

To be sure, we ought to be able to appreciate the desire that moves us to cling to life. "A living dog is better than a dead lion," Qoheleth says (Eccles. 9:4), articulating succinctly the thirst for more life. He is not entirely wrong, since, after all, only the living can aim at anything more than living. Nevertheless, to take survival as our primary goal — however necessary at times in a seemingly Hobbesian world — does not express the full dignity of our humanity. A virtuous commitment to the indefinite prolongation of life cannot be founded merely on the narcissistic desire to survive — not, at least, without losing the virtues of a complete life that has shape and not just duration.

⊠   ⊠   ⊠

There are complications here, however, that we should not too quickly or too easily unravel. Perhaps the desire for an indefinitely extended life may have its own virtuous character. Perhaps it can take root in the virtue of love. Indeed, this is, I believe, the strongest argument for attempts to retard aging and prolong life indefinitely. Somewhat to my own surprise, I find that it makes me hesitant — and should make us hesitant — to dismiss too quickly the desire to retard aging. Even if there are deep problems with this desire — even if, were the desire satisfied, we would lose the kind of wholeness given by the shape of what I have called a "complete life" — something more than mere narcissism may be at work in this desire. That something more is the virtue of love.

How love might elicit from us a desire to extend life is captured beautifully in John Hall Wheelock's poem, "Song on Reaching Seventy."[21] "Shall not a man sing as the night comes on?" the poet asks. And remembering how — as the quiet of evening descends

---

21. John Hall Wheelock, "Song on Reaching Seventy," in *This Blessed Earth: New and Selected Poems, 1927-1977* (New York: Charles Scribner's Sons, 1978), pp. 56-57.

but before all is silence — he has heard a thrush "Lift up his heart against the menacing night," he is moved to reflect on the sweetness of life.

> *Oh, now*
> *Before the coming of a greater night*
> *How bitterly sweet and dear*
> *All things have grown! How shall we bear the brunt,*
> *The fury and joy of every sound and sight,*
> *Now almost cruelly fierce with all delight.*

The delights of the natural world come unbidden to his mind: the sun making its way through the clouds of dawn; that sun's light still piercing the clouds at its evening burial; a pool of rain; the flight of a bat; the cock pheasant's morning call. "Oh, every sight and sound has meaning now."

Still more, he calls to mind those to whom he is closely tied in love — so closely tied that even the thought of his beloved can almost make him afraid. It is like looking at the sun and being blinded by truth, the truth of a longing that will not be quieted.

> *Age will look into the face of youth*
> *With longing, over a gulf not to be crossed.*
> *Oh, joy that is almost pain, pain that is joy,*
> *Unimaginable to the younger man or boy.*

Thus, "Song on Reaching Seventy" tells of a longing that never disappears, that is never quite fulfilled — uniting sweetness and heartache.

We might say, of course, that the "joy that is almost pain" and the "pain that is joy" could not be so rich, ambivalent, and deeply moving an experience were it not that life moves relentlessly through its stages toward its appointed end. We might say — and this is a profound truth not to be forgotten — that were the poet magically to cross back over that "gulf not to be crossed," his longing would remain "unstilled." All true. Yet, we cannot deny the power of love.

To love another is to affirm that person's being and well-being. Not just well-being, but the sheer goodness of the loved one's existence. To love another is to say (in Josef Pieper's phrase) "it's good that you exist," repeating the Creator's own affirmation.[22] Anyone who has loved must therefore feel the force of the poet's concluding plea.

> *Great night, hold back*
> *A little longer yet your mountainous, black*
> *Waters of darkness, from this shore, . . .*
> *The haunt of love and pain,*
> *Which we must leave, whether we would or not,*
> *And where we shall not come again.*
> *More time — oh, but a little more,*
> *Till, stretched to the limits of being, the taut heart break,*
> *Bursting the bonds of breath.*

And of course, for anyone who loves, for as long as he loves, it may continue to make sense to say, "More time — oh, but a little more." We should, therefore, be able to understand the thirst that drives research aimed at retarding or, even, overcoming the aging process. If aging is, in one sense, built into our nature, the desire to live more (and more) is, in another sense, equally natural for people formed by the virtue of love.

If, despite the power of such love, there is good reason not to aim at extending our life span indefinitely, it cannot be that the delights the poet mentions are unworthy of our deep affection. Nor, I suspect, can we simply assert that all of us must find the virtues of a "complete life" more compelling than "more life." It must rather be that there is yet more to being human than the poet has discerned

---

22. Josef Pieper, *Faith, Hope, Love* (San Francisco: Ignatius Press, 1997), p. 164.

and that the beauties of more life — sweet as they are — cannot, as St. Augustine puts it, catch the heart and hold it still. It must be that our freedom to step beyond nature's limits is itself part of our nature and will not rest content with more of this life, however long extended. Hence, knowing how endless (and legitimate) is our thirst for more life, God places cherubim with flaming brands to bar any return to paradise, lest humankind should eat of the tree of life and live — more of the same life — forever. In the end, "more time" would not quench the thirst that drives us to look for ways to retard aging. We need a fuller conception of our humanity and a deeper and richer understanding of love — one that is shaped by patience and hope in the struggle to understand what, really, is good for us.

CHAPTER TWO

Transitional Humanity

....

*It is a loathsome and cruel trick that nature takes such an exqui-
sitely wondrous creation as the human brain and imprisons it
inside the weak, inefficient, fragile, and short-lived structure that is
the human body. . . . The body you now inhabit, however remarkable
it may be, is not the product of intelligent design. It was not created
for any purpose other than survival and reproduction.*

Mike Treder, "Emancipation from Death"

*They who wait for the LORD shall renew their strength,
        they shall mount up with wings like eagles,
they shall run and not be weary,
        they shall walk and not faint.*

Isaiah 40:31

....

An earlier version of this chapter appeared as "Transitional Humanity" in *The New Atlantis*
31 (Spring 2011): 82-92.

"IF YOU'RE UNDER age 30, it is likely that you will be able to live as long as you want."[1] That was the message Ronald Bailey took away from a longevity summit convened in November 2009. Bringing together "scientists, entrepreneurs, and visionaries" — all of them dedicated to achieving indefinite extension of human life within the next few decades — the summit included reports on a wide range of possible means to that goal. The desirability of the goal was, of course, taken for granted.

The idea is to survive long enough to be around when hoped-for technological advances will make possible indefinite extension of life. Bailey reports that, at the longevity summit, Ray Kurzweil, one of the visionary thinkers committed to this goal, stated that within roughly fifteen years we may have advanced to a point where we can add "more than one year of longevity per year to remaining life expectancy" — thereby getting out in front of time's relentless arrow. This is what Aubrey de Grey has characterized as "longevity escape velocity": when one's projected date of death moves farther away rather than nearer. The same idea is captured in the subtitle of the book *Fantastic Voyage,* coauthored by Kurzweil and Terry Grossman: *Live Long Enough to Live Forever.*[2]

For the moment, this means taking some rather conventional steps — diet, exercise, stress reduction — though, to be sure, taking them with intensity. But if we are fortunate, these steps will keep us in good health into a coming era of biotechnological advance, in which regenerative medicine can ceaselessly repair the accumulated damage in our bodies that is the mark of aging. This repair may take many forms — chromosome replacement, regenerative medicine using cloned stem cells, drugs that mimic the effects of caloric restriction or that lengthen telomeres. Finally, these forms of biological repair may, we are told, help us survive

1. Ronald Bailey, "The Methuselah Manifesto: Witnessing the Launch of Immortality, Inc.?" Online at http://reason.com/archives/2009/11/17/the-methuselah-manifesto. Accessed September 12, 2010.

2. Ray Kurzweil and Terry Grossman, *Fantastic Voyage: Live Long Enough to Live Forever* (Emmaus, PA: Rodale, Inc., 2004).

into a time when the human body as we know it will have become obsolete — a time in which it will be possible to map the brain and preserve its information (and, thereby, our identity) in ways no longer dependent on organic bodies, which can then give way to a "virtual" existence.[3]

These hopes and expectations are captured succinctly in the Transhumanist Declaration, first drawn up in 1998 and most recently revised in 2009: "We envision the possibility of broadening human potential by overcoming aging, cognitive shortcomings, involuntary suffering, and our confinement to planet Earth."[4] Were this vision actually to play out in our history, we would live through a transitional humanity on its way to something that would truly deserve to be called posthumanity. I confess to doubting the likelihood of at least a good bit of what is promised by such visionaries, but we will not waste our time if we think about their hopes. For even if much of this turns out to be a pipe dream, the fact that some among us — how many I'm not sure — think it desirable is reason enough for us to pay attention. What we hope for tells us a great deal about who we are.

Some of these attempts to extend life probably fall under the rubric of "enhancement," a by now well-worn topic in bioethical discussion of issues such as cosmetic surgery, mood brightening drugs, and "designer" babies. Once our target becomes not only the average but also the maximum life span, however, it becomes harder to think that we are simply enhancing capacities already in place. On the contrary, we are aiming at something genuinely new, something hard to contemplate or evaluate with our normal ways of thinking, focused, as they are, simply on benefits and harms. We are forced to think about the kind of people we are and should strive to be — about what will truly help us to flour-

3. Raymond Kurzweil, "Human Body Version 2.0," in Immortality Institute, *The Scientific Conquest of Death: Essays on Infinite Lifespans* (Buenos Aires: LibrosEnRed, 2004), pp. 93-106. Online at http://www.imminst.org/SCOD.pdf. Accessed September 22, 2010.

4. "Transhumanist Declaration." Online at http://humanityplus.org/learn/transhumanist-declaration. Accessed September 30, 2010.

ish as human beings. Most importantly, perhaps, we must come to terms with our nature as organisms, as bodies that limit us in countless ways and limit our days. Is that just an unfortunate (and, we may hope, temporary) fact, to be overcome first in ageless, organic bodies and then even in virtual, inorganic ones? Or shall we say, as the Creator of animals and man does in Genesis, that this embodied life is "very good"?

⌛   ⌛   ⌛

Katherine Hayles has captured the idea of posthumanity nicely, characterizing it as assuming

1   that "informational patterns" (such as those in the human brain) are more important than their "material instantiation" (in the brain itself);
2   that consciousness is an epiphenomenon caused by and reducible to brain activity;
3   that the body is our first prosthesis (i.e., something used by the self rather than integral to our selfhood); and
4   that there is no essential difference between bodies and computer simulations, between organisms and mechanisms.[5]

Pushed to its limits, the idea is that we should think of the computer as a model for humanity and think of life itself as (at least potentially) artificial.[6] We ourselves, therefore, are essentially patterns of information. For the time being those patterns are housed in bodies — though, alas, bodies that age — which serve as our prostheses, as artificial limbs used by our brains. A day may come, however, when the particular information pattern that is you or

---

5. N. Katherine Hayles, *How We Became Posthuman: Virtual Bodies in Cybernetics, Literature, and Informatics* (Chicago and London: University of Chicago Press, 1999), pp. 2-3.

6. Ellen Ullman, "Programming the Post-Human," *Harper's Magazine* 305 (October 2002): 62-63.

me can be carried by some new prosthesis, a "body" that, being inorganic, will not age and will offer us the chance for a kind of immortality. Indeed, if the information stored in the brain could somehow be extracted and transferred to a computer, we might even imagine making backup copies of ourselves. This would, in Mike Treder's words, "really make us effectively immortal, as we could store copies of ourselves in places all over the solar system, the galaxy, or, eventually, even beyond."[7]

Although I doubt the feasibility of such visions and do not expect them to be realized, I do not think they are as strange or unusual as one might at first suppose. Already in the first decades of the twentieth century, visionary thinkers such as H. G. Wells, George Bernard Shaw, J. B. S. Haldane, and Julian Huxley thought seriously — and optimistically — about the pursuit of immortality. C. S. Lewis was less optimistic, and his alternative vision pinpoints the crucial disagreements.

In *That Hideous Strength,* Lewis envisioned a research institute, the National Institute of Co-ordinated Experiments (N.I.C.E.), whose research aims, though not its methods, anticipate visions of post-humanity.[8] The leaders of N.I.C.E. believe that the modern scientific project of controlling nature has reached a point at which humanity itself must now become yet another natural object to be reshaped in service of our desires. This project involves the overcoming of all organic life. Professor Filostrato, a physiologist, looks forward to a day when, for instance, artificial metal trees will replace living ones. This strikes him as a far more rational approach. If one tires of a tree in one place, one simply has it moved to a new location. "It never dies. No leaves to fall, no twigs, no birds building nests, no muck and mess."[9]

7. Mike Treder, "Emancipation from Death," in Immortality Institute, *The Scientific Conquest of Death,* p. 191. Online at http://www.imminst.org/SCOD.pdf. Accessed September 22, 2010.

8. C. S. Lewis, *That Hideous Strength: A Modern Fairy-Tale for Grown-Ups* (New York: Macmillan, 1965).

9. Lewis, *That Hideous Strength,* p. 172.

Applied to humanity, the lesson is clear. Organic life, having done its work in producing mind, is no longer needed. Death must be overcome and reproduction transformed into a technological project. For Lewis, of course, this is hardly a desirable future, and N.I.C.E. is satirized throughout *That Hideous Strength*. Beyond and beneath the satire, however, is a serious concern. "Dreams of the far future destiny of man were dragging up from its shallow and unquiet grave the old dream of Man as God."[10] Over against that old dream Lewis sets a vision of human dignity that accepts the limits of organic life — including aging and death — as limits to be affirmed and honored. Human beings are not simply isolated principles of will committed to indefinite self-transcendence.

The alternatives and the fundamental argument remain much the same today. Since the time of those visionary thinkers in the early decades of the twentieth century we have increasingly taught ourselves to think in ways that cohere with transhumanist aims. For example, it has become quite common (especially in discussions about the beginning and the end of life) to distinguish between the class of *human beings* and a narrower class of *persons* (who are thought to be characterized by certain capacities dependent upon the higher, neocortical functions of the brain). If one thinks that way, and if one thinks it is persons that really matter, one might say with Roland Puccetti that "conquest of death" requires "indefinite prolongation of neocortical function."[11] For without such function, Puccetti thinks, one's continued existence would have no value.

The catch is, of course, that for now a body is required to sustain those brain functions, and that body will grow old and, eventually, die. "But must we have bodies?" Puccetti thinks not. "[A]n intact human brain kept *in vitro* but nourished by a properly oxygenated and glucose-supplied blood flow mechanically pumped into it through

10. Lewis, *That Hideous Strength*, p. 203.

11. Roland Puccetti, "The Conquest of Death," in *Language, Metaphysics, and Death*, ed. John Donnelly (New York: Fordham University Press, 1978), p. 166.

the severed arteries could support conscious life."[12] (This is exactly the stage of technological experiment to which N.I.C.E. has advanced in Lewis's story.) Of course, such an isolated brain, though it could have memories of its past (bodily) history, could have no future — could not continue to act and engage the world — unless it had some prosthesis, some new "body" through which to carry on exchange with its surrounding environment. But if this were a material body of the sort we now inhabit, it would still age and die. Hence, Puccetti is drawn to hope for something different. "The idea of escaping the evolutionary limitations of our present bodies by having our brains transplanted at postmaturity into bodies which, being inorganic, do not age or deteriorate, has a prima facie attractiveness about it."[13]

This vision of personhood draws on deeper roots in the modern liberal tradition, which has taught us to think of ourselves as *possessing* rather than *being* a body. "Although," as Katherine Hayles notes, "in many ways the posthuman deconstructs the liberal humanist subject, it . . . shares with its predecessor an emphasis on cognition rather than embodiment."[14] And, as Francis Fukuyama observes, Immanuel Kant believed that the moral norms authorized by his ethical theory would apply not just to human beings — embodied creatures of a certain sort — but also to any and all rational agents.[15] The body both locates and, simultaneously, limits us. Desire is bound to time and place, to the nature of organic life, and cannot be entirely free. It becomes apparent, therefore, that the desire to live forever is, in fact, a desire to be located "everywhere and nowhere."[16] The modern alternative, which Kant so brilliantly developed, unfetters desire and focuses on the freedom of disembodied will to

---

12. Puccetti, "The Conquest of Death," p. 169.
13. Puccetti, "The Conquest of Death," p. 170.
14. Hayles, *How We Became Posthuman*, p. 5.
15. Francis Fukuyama, *Our Posthuman Future* (New York: Farrar, Straus and Giroux, 2002), p. 119.
16. Stephen R. L. Clark, *How to Live Forever: Science Fiction and Philosophy* (London and New York: Routledge, 1995), p. 47.

realize itself over against all the ordinary marks (sex, kinship ties, stages of life) of human, personal identity.

But the target of transhumanists is not simply death. More precisely, the target is death we have not chosen. The introduction to the Immortality Institute's reader, *The Scientific Conquest of Death*, puts it succinctly: "The mission of the Immortality Institute is to conquer the blight of involuntary death."[17] Thus, the philosopher John Gray gets it just right when he says: "The pursuit of immortality through science is only incidentally a project aiming to defeat death. At bottom it is an attempt to escape contingency and mystery."[18] Not to be in control, to suffer the limits of a fate we have not chosen — that is the enemy. The goal of indefinite life-extension is not so much in service of particular loves or projects as it is in service of one indefinitely expansive desire — to become agents who are not at the mercy of forces beyond our own control, in particular, the forces of decline and decay that are built into the very nature of organic life.

⊠   ⊠   ⊠

This desire draws us into thinking of ourselves in a way that misses important aspects of our humanity. The posthumanist vision begins with a thoroughgoing commitment to materialistic reductionism, in order, then, to reimagine human beings as immaterial — as utterly disembodied. We are, according to this view, what our brains do. Mind and personal identity are located in the pattern of information housed in the brain, and our memories and emotions are simply the behavior of its nerve cells. Having reduced mind to that, we can then imagine the possibility of transferring it to a computer program, where the "self" would remain in entirely immaterial form.

Philosopher Alva Noë has noted that this way of thinking sup-

---

17. Immortality Institute, *The Scientific Conquest of Death*, p. 7. Online at http://www. imminst.org/SCOD.pdf. Accessed September 22, 2010.

18. John Gray, *The Immortalization Commission: Science and the Strange Quest to Cheat Death* (New York: Farrar, Straus and Giroux, 2011), p. 213.

poses that consciousness is a process internal to the brain in the way digestion is to the stomach, and he vividly captures what this means for our conception of humanity: "What are we then? If the truth be told, we are brains in vats on life support. . . . Our skulls are the vats and our bodies the life-support systems that keep us going."[19] I will follow him here in noting three closely related reasons why this way of thinking about the identity of human persons cannot be adequate.

Brains in vats with bodies for life-support systems, for whom consciousness is more like digestion than dancing, cannot have our experience of being purposive agents in the world. For, as Noë puts it, consciousness is something we achieve; it is the way we live in and respond to our surrounding world, not something that just happens to us or in us. Human beings — in fact, living organisms generally — are not simply mechanisms but are relational from the start. Even so simple a being as a bacterium can be understood only when we "appreciate its integrity as an individual agent, as a bearer of interests and needs." It "has a world; that is to say, it has a relationship with its surroundings."[20] Hence, rather than thinking of a bacterium as just a place where physical and chemical processes take place, we have to discern "its primitive agency, its possession of interests, needs, and point of view" — which is to say, its "incipient mindfulness."[21] Surely, then, the more complex organism that is a human being is not simply a mechanical process to be understood in terms of physics and chemistry alone. Even if one eliminates all teleology from the universe and supposes that our world and its evolutionary history have no purpose, it seems to have produced living beings who do have purposes and who act as agents in the world.

---

19. Alva Noë, *Out of Our Heads: Why You Are Not Your Brain, and Other Lessons from the Biology of Consciousness* (New York: Hill and Wang, 2009), p. 4.

20. Noë, *Out of Our Heads*, p. 40. For a somewhat fuller depiction of the character of organic life, a depiction influenced by the thought of Hans Jonas, see chapter 2 of Gilbert Meilaender, *Neither Beast nor God: The Dignity of the Human Person* (New York and London: Encounter Books, 2009).

21. Noë, *Out of Our Heads*, p. 41.

A second way to come at this same point is to remind ourselves that it is not the brain that thinks, though we may often talk in ways which suggest that it is. After all, we also often talk as if we see with our eyes, when, in fact, it is the living being who sees, not simply a pair of eyes. More than a century ago, William James already noted that we should not think of the brain producing thought in the way a teakettle produces steam. Rather, James suggested, we might think of how the keys of an organ allow wind to enter its pipes, producing "the voices of the various pipes," but the keys do not produce the wind itself or the sounds.[22] Or, to take an analogy offered by philosopher Stephen Clark: If we damage the internal workings of a television set, the programs shown will be affected. That does not mean, however, that it is the television that is generating those programs.[23]

As sight is not located in the optic nerve, so thought is not located in the brain. Hence, Noë argues, when we picture the brain as somehow examining its own contents in order to process that information (and, in effect, think about itself), we tacitly smuggle into the picture something else, some subject that transcends itself. But that's what consciousness is! "The mind is not in the head," and the self-conscious, self-transcending subject is constantly engaging with, living in, and responding to the world around him.[24] There, and not in the brain's nerve cells, is the thinker.

Finally, suppose we thought it possible to upload into a computer the pattern of information that constitutes our brain, thereby preserving our identity in a new form. In thinking that way, we adopt toward ourselves and others a position of detachment — as if "we" simply were, without remainder, a physiological pattern of behavior that could be observed and charted. But this is a theory that cannot be lived. We cannot think about ourselves or others from that

---

22. William James, "Human Immortality," the Ingersoll Lecture for 1898. Available online at http://www.religion-online.org/showchapter.asp?title=541&C=624.

23. Clark, *How to Live Forever*, p. 115.

24. Noë, *Out of Our Heads*, p. 164.

detached standpoint while simultaneously sharing life with them as we do. To see this, we need only imagine the impossibility of loving another person while, at the same time, trying to think about ourselves loving them. Lover and beloved share a world, and in that world they know each other as mindful persons, not as patterns of behavior. "Like the baby in relation to her mother, we are involved with each other. It is our joint cohabitation that secures our living consciousness for each other."[25] To suppose that we could preserve our identity in the form of a computerized pattern of information is to adopt toward ourselves the kind of detached standpoint that loses this living, bodily engagement with the world that simply *is* the mindful self. Hence, we cannot coherently think of ourselves in the way the posthumanist project recommends.

⌧   ⌧   ⌧

These epistemological failings should spur us to anticipate related moral failings. If the transhumanist project were the only route to more life, to an indefinitely prolonged existence, the price of success might be the loss of our humanity. Even on purely naturalistic grounds we might wonder whether the indefinitely extended existence for which transhumanists hope does not lose important aspects of a characteristically human life — in particular, its shape and contours. To have parents, as we all do — or to be the parent of sons and daughters, as many of us are — is to be embedded in a series of temporal relationships that involve not only coming into being but also going out of being. The relation between the generations shapes a life in which moments of time are not simply identical. Some are more "moment-ous" than others, giving to life a trajectory that has a beginning, middle, and end.

Thus, our lives have a narrative shape, making our experience something other than a succession of bare, momentary presents.

25. Noë, *Out of Our Heads,* p. 33.

This means that growing old is not just a matter of biology; it has social, psychic, and religious dimensions. The philosopher Larry Temkin makes this point in an arresting thought experiment: "As things stand today, the physical, psychological, and experiential gap between a grandmother at 60, a mother at 35, and a daughter at 9 is enormous. But the physical, psychological, and experiential gaps between a grandmother at 10,060, a mother at 10,035, and a daughter at 10,009 would be practically inconsequential."[26] Memory and anticipation have their primary bodily location in our connection to our parents and our children, and it is hard to know what human experience would look or feel like — or whether it would really be *human* experience — were our lives not embedded in the bonds that produce stages within life and give the whole of it a narrative shape.

One very old way of depicting that shape is to picture life as a banquet, with a succession of courses through which one proceeds — and also, to be sure, having a stopping point beyond which the banquet cannot be prolonged without destroying its pleasure. Both host and guest at such a banquet must be able to acknowledge limits — recognizing that, while these limits may suffuse the end of the banquet or even the whole of it with a touch of fragility and sadness, they cannot destroy its goodness. Consider David H. Smith's depiction of the good host.

> A couple invite friends to dinner. Food and drink are pleasant; the conversation bubbles. The good host is hospitable and courteous to his guest, no matter what his shifts in mood. But there comes a time when the party "winds down" — a time to acknowledge that the evening is over. At that point, not easily determined by clock, conversation, or basal metabolism, the good host does not press his guest to stay but lets him go. Indeed he may have to signal that it is acceptable to leave. A good host will never be sure of his timing and will never kick out

26. Larry Temkin, "Is Living Longer Living Better?" in *Enhancing Human Capacities*, ed. Julian Savulescu, Ruud ter Meulen, and Guy Kahane (Malden, MA: Wiley-Blackwell, 2011), pp. 362-63.

his guest. His jurisdiction over the guest is limited to taking care and permitting departure.[27]

When we think of life as such a banquet, a death that comes neither too soon nor too late — neither when the banquet is just getting started nor long after all have eaten their fill — may be thought fitting. It is, at least, recognizably human in a way that posthumanist visions may not be. Moreover, this picture of a complete human life, with its acknowledgment and even affirmation of human limits, will have an undeniable nobility that is displayed in patience, humility, and gratitude. Daniel Callahan offers a nice example that captures the beauty in such patience.

> I once heard someone's elderly grandfather described as a man of great energy and activity who, as he aged, had to live, because of illness and aging, within a smaller and smaller physical radius. Yet, even as that radius narrowed, first to the yard he could not leave, then to the house he could not leave, then to the room he could not leave, and finally to the bed he could not leave, he adapted to each smaller world, making of it with good cheer whatever was possible. An imaginative flower arranger I once heard said that the secret lies in learning how to work with the material at hand, not longing for flowers not available. He then demonstrated what he meant by fashioning a wonderful arrangement from roadside weeds.[28]

Thus, patience to run the course of life's banquet need not be simply resignation. It can, at its best, make possible genuine freedom even within the necessities that constrain us.

One aspect of our nature is, however, missing from such a vision of life's banquet: namely, the eros that longs for God. Grounded in

---

27. David H. Smith, *Health and Medicine in the Anglican Tradition* (New York: Crossroad, 1986), p. 52.

28. Daniel Callahan, *The Troubled Dream of Life: Living with Mortality* (New York: Simon & Schuster, 1993), p. 138.

our freedom to transcend the natural course of organic life, this eros suggests a sense in which the banquet of life is never quite complete. When human life, in all its limits and vulnerability, remains open to the divine life, we can begin to see the power and meaning of the virtue of hope, which is quite different from transhumanist optimism about the future. Hope's ground is, to take up theologian David Kelsey's term, "eccentric."[29] It looks for completion not to the natural course of life, nor to the achievements of human progress or history, but to the genuinely creative and re-creative power that is God's.

⛞   ⛞   ⛞

"We are the creature that hopes," Hugh Heclo writes.[30] The importance — perhaps the necessity — of hope for human life has long been known. The Victorian painter G. F. Watts's *Hope* depicts a blindfolded woman holding a broken lyre on which only one string remains; yet, that one string is evidently intended to evoke hope in those who view the painting, hope that there is music still to be made.[31] Watts is, of course, drawing on classical mythology's depiction of Pandora's jar, in which only hope remained after she had released into the world the evils inside. Whatever precisely the myth means — and it may mean many things — hope can help us to flourish only if it is something other than mere expectation, optimism, or confidence. What we hope for tells us a good bit about who we are.

Confidence in progress has marked the modern period. The French *philosophe* Nicolas de Condorcet, one of the great thinkers of the Enlightenment, memorably expressed this confident

29. David H. Kelsey, *Eccentric Existence: A Theological Anthropology*, vol. 1 (Louisville: Westminster John Knox Press, 2009).

30. Hugh Heclo, *On Thinking Institutionally* (Boulder and London: Paradigm Publishers, 2008), p. 194.

31. For Watts's painting, see: http://www.artmagick.com/pictures/picture. aspx?id=5875&ame=hope.

expectation in his *Sketch for a Historical Picture of the Progress of the Human Mind*. (It is one of the ironies of history that he had to complete it while hiding from leaders of the Revolution, which had begun to devour its children.)

> We feel that the progress of preventive medicine as a preservative, made more effective by the progress of reason and social order, will eventually banish communicable or contagious illnesses and those diseases in general that originate in climate, food, and the nature of work. It would not be difficult to prove that this hope should extend to almost all other diseases, whose more remote causes will eventually be recognized. Would it be absurd now to suppose that the improvement of the human race should be regarded as capable of unlimited progress? That a time will come when death would result only from extraordinary accidents or the more and more gradual wearing out of vitality, and that, finally, the duration of the average interval between birth and wearing out has itself no specific limit whatsoever?[32]

The historian Carl Becker famously argued that, despite some obvious differences, there was significant continuity between a faith such as Condorcet's in a good ending and the hope a thirteenth-century thinker such as Thomas Aquinas had for future salvation.[33]

Where Becker was struck by continuities, we might, though, be more impressed by differences. Enlightenment thinkers such as Condorcet placed their hope not in God but in future generations of humanity — in, that is, more of the same. "Posterity would complete what the past and the present had begun."[34] This is not a minor difference, for the hope in posterity was a confidence in human capacities and possibilities — in the expectation that we ourselves could overcome the fragility and vulnerability of human

---

32. Nicolas de Condorcet, *The Future Progress of the Human Mind*. http://www.fordham.edu/halsall/mod/condorcet-progress.html.

33. Carl L. Becker, *The Heavenly City of the Eighteenth-Century Philosophers* (New Haven: Yale University Press, 1932), see especially chapter 4, "The Uses of Posterity."

34. Becker, *The Heavenly City of the Eighteenth-Century Philosophers*, p. 129.

life. That sort of confident expectation about our future historical accomplishments loses something that was once central to — and may still be needed for — the virtue of hope.

St. Thomas distinguishes between a *comprehensor* and a *viator.* A *comprehensor* possesses — and cannot lose — the happiness he desires. A *viator,* by contrast, is always and only on the way to that desired end. Hence, we can hope only for what is not yet a permanent and present condition. Hope is possible only for those for whom life, however long, always seems less than complete — "those who are still en route" *(in viatoribus).*[35]

En route to what? How we answer that question makes an enormous difference in how we understand hope. For Aquinas — as for the Christian tradition on which he drew — what human beings hope for is a lasting union with the God who has shared our vulnerability and overcome it. Only the beauty and goodness of this God can catch the heart and hold it still, answering its deepest desire. Such Christian hope for beatitude is not a desire for more of this life, wonderful though it is; nor is it a desire even for a "complete life," however precisely we picture its shape; nor is it a desire for any human or posthuman future that we ourselves might fashion. Only if we were to stifle the human eros for God could we suppose that an extended longevity of our own making could ever lead us to imagine that we had arrived at the desired goal.

The relentless temporality of human life means that we are always incomplete, always *in viatoribus,* always on the way. Hope is the virtue that sustains us on the way toward the divine beauty and goodness — protecting us against a presumption which supposes that any of us could here and now become a *comprehensor,* as if an indefinitely extended earthly life, whether organic or virtual, could quench our longing. And protecting us also against despair, against the temptation to make of our vulnerability a virtue. Hope moves us to desire something more than life's banquet, sumptuous as it

---

35. *Summa Theologiae,* IIaIIae, q. 18, a. 3.

may be, something other than just indefinitely more of the same life, and something more than the achievement of "longevity escape velocity." It enables us to wait for the strength to run and not be weary, to walk and not faint — a strength no research project can produce and which can only be received as a gift.

CHAPTER THREE

Hoping to Live Forever

....

A reasonably endowed, reasonably well-intentioned man can walk through the world's great kitchen from end to end and arrive at the back door hungry.

Wallace Stegner, *The Spectator Bird*

Further up and further in.

C. S. Lewis, *The Last Battle*

ONE OF THE ironies of our cultural circumstances is that at the very same time when research proceeds on many fronts aimed at retarding aging and extending life indefinitely, others argue that an immortal life would be an undesirable life. And, of course, if their arguments are persuasive, we would have good reason to draw back from the project of anti-aging research.

To be sure, we are not the first to puzzle over such conflicting impulses. George Bernard Shaw wrote a cycle of plays called *Back to Methuselah: A Metabiological Pentateuch.* The first of the plays is set in the Garden of Eden and titled (unsurprisingly) "In the Beginning." In it Adam learns from Eve news that she herself had gotten from the serpent — namely, that they need not live forever. And he responds with relief and delight:

> What! Eve: do not play with me about this. If only there may be an end some day and yet no end! If only I can be relieved of the horror of having to endure myself for ever! If only the care of this terrible garden may pass on to some other gardener! If only the sentinel set by the Voice can be relieved! If only the rest and sleep that enable me to bear it from day to day could grow after many years into an eternal rest, an eternal sleep, then I could face my days, however long they may last. Only, there must be some end, some end: I am not strong enough to bear eternity.[1]

Later in the play Adam expresses a similar sentiment to Cain, who, having killed his brother Abel, asks his parents who invented death. And Adam replies:

> Be reasonable, boy. Could you bear to live for ever? You think you could, because you know that you will never have to make your thought good. But I have known what it is to sit and brood under the terror of eternity, of immortality. Think of it, man: to have no escape! To be Adam, Adam,

1. George Bernard Shaw, *Back to Methuselah: A Metabiological Pentateuch,* "The World's Classics" rev. ed. with Postscript (New York and London: Oxford University Press, 1947), pp. 10-11.

Adam through more days than there are grains of sand by the two rivers, and then be as far from the end as ever! I, who have so much in me that I hate and long to cast off! Be thankful to your parents, who enabled you to hand on your burden to new and better men, and won for you an eternal rest; for it was we who invented death.[2]

It is worth noting that Adam does not wish to die immediately; indeed, he decides to live for one thousand years before dying. Nor does he want human life to cease. But it is the species, not the individual, for whose survival he hopes. As Eve says to Adam, "You may die when I have made another Adam. Not before. But then, as soon as you like."[3] She recognizes, it seems, the close connection between reproduction and death.

Shaw's "Metabiological Pentateuch" envisions possibilities akin to what we now call transhumanism and hopes for a future in which the human species, surviving indefinitely, becomes something like pure mind. As Shaw put it in a postscript written twenty-five years after the first publication of the play cycle, "Immortality is natural, death only an artifice to make it bearable as a burden and get rid of its garments of flesh as they wear out."[4] But any immortality Shaw was willing to hope for required, in William Irvine's words, "the somewhat cheerless universality of pure thought."[5] Life as we now experience it would, he believed, be unutterably tedious were it to extend indefinitely. To live forever as we live now would be not paradise but a curse — "analogous to the experience of severe insomnia," as the philosopher Christine Overall puts it.[6]

⊠   ⊠   ⊠

2. Shaw, *Back to Methuselah,* p. 30.
3. Shaw, *Back to Methuselah,* pp. 12-13.
4. Shaw, Postscript to *Back to Methuselah,* p. 255.
5. William Irvine, *The Universe of G. B. S.* (New York: Macmillan, 1949), p. 317.
6. Christine Overall, *Aging, Death and Human Longevity: A Philosophical Inquiry* (Berkeley: University of California Press, 2003), p. 143.

More recently, the case against living forever — in particular, the argument that to do so would be tedious and boring — has been made by various thinkers, perhaps most notably the philosopher Bernard Williams. To attend to his argument is to see that there is no metaphysically neutral ground from which to discuss whether an immortal life could be satisfying. We cannot know what we think of attempts to retard aging or prolong our lives indefinitely unless we know what a human being is and what it would mean for human beings to flourish.

In "The Makropulos Case: Reflections on the Tedium of Immortality," Williams begins by reflecting on a play by Karel Capek about a woman named Elina Makropulos.[7] At age 42 she had been given an elixir by her physician father, and as the play unfolds she is now 342 and facing a momentous choice. Because each dose of the elixir gives three hundred additional years of life, she has come to the time when she must decide whether to drink it again and, so to speak, renew the contract. She refuses and, as a consequence, dies — reasonably enough in Williams's view. "Her unending life has," he writes, "come to a state of boredom, indifference and coldness."[8]

Whatever might be fulfilling for other sorts of beings, there can, Williams thinks, be no good reason "for living eternally a human life."[9] Human lives are limited in a variety of ways, giving to each of us a distinct character. And even if the range of possible experiences is enormous, not all such experiences can be satisfying or fulfilling for someone whose character has taken a particular shape and form. Becoming a person of a certain sort does not only mean growth and expansion of one's possibilities; it also means closing some doors precisely in order to step through others. To be someone, I must eschew the attempt to be everyone — and, being someone in particular, I can no longer take interest

---

7. Bernard Williams, "The Makropulos Case: Reflections on the Tedium of Immortality," in *Problems of the Self* (Cambridge: Cambridge University Press, 1973), pp. 82-100.

8. Williams, "The Makropulos Case," p. 82.

9. Williams, "The Makropulos Case," p. 89.

in just anything, however good it may be in principle. That is the heart of Williams's argument.

This is a claim worth thinking about from several different angles. Is it true, in the first place, that a finite human being, whose character has taken a certain form and shape, must eventually run out of things or experiences that engage his interest? Charles Taliaferro, also a philosopher, has distinguished "time enclosed goods" from "non-time enclosed goods."[10] The enjoyment of the former depends in part precisely on the fact that they do not last forever. Taliaferro's example: a meal. However good and pleasurable the meal, it would lose its value if continued indefinitely. The meal has a sequence of courses (as we think of life having stages), and its goodness requires that we pass through those courses and complete the meal. Hence, no meal, however sumptuous, could delight us forever.

That is true of any single meal. But, of course, if we allow ourselves certain beliefs, we may imagine an endlessly extended existence in which there is, as Taliaferro puts it, "a great, perhaps indefinite variety or alteration of time enclosed goods."[11] Indeed, Williams's concept of boredom seems fundamentally mistaken. As Steven Horrobin notes, "We are not bored *simpliciter.* Boredom without reference *to something we would rather be doing* is meaningless."[12] That is to say, being bored with some good or other presupposes continued interest in and desire for another of the indefinite variety of goods to which Taliaferro refers.

I myself am not even certain that indefinite variety is needed. Must being a person of a distinct character (as Williams puts it) subvert our capacity to appreciate — time and again — the beauty of sunrise, the tranquility of twilight, the marvel of a child's first steps,

---

10. Charles Taliaferro, "Why We Need Immortality," *Modern Theology* 6, no. 4 (July 1990): 368.

11. Taliaferro, "Why We Need Immortality," p. 369.

12. Steven Horrobin, "The Value of Life Extension to Persons as Conatively Driven Processes," in *Enhancing Human Capacities,* ed. Julian Savulescu, Ruud ter Meulen, and Guy Kahane (Malden, MA: Wiley-Blackwell, 2011), p. 430.

or the savoring of a good story? If such goods begin someday to bore us, perhaps the problem is that we have not yet fully developed the sort of character a human being ought to have or be. If we find them tedious, it may be not that these experiences have failed us but that we have failed them. That is a possible rejoinder to Williams.

Still, that response may not take seriously enough his insistence that we think through what it means to be limited in the ways that human beings are. Perhaps we are so constituted that even life's beauties and delights cannot indefinitely and fully engage us. That may be. What follows from that, however, is not so clear. It could mean simply, as Williams supposes, that human beings are not meant to live forever. Or it could mean that these beauties and delights are meant less to fulfill our desires than to invite us through and beyond them to some yet more satisfying good. Thus, any Augustinian would happily grant that finite beauties cannot bear the whole weight of the heart's longing, for they are shafts of the divine glory intended to direct our desire to what Taliaferro calls "some singular non-time enclosed good" — that is, to draw us to God.[13]

The 1993 movie *Groundhog Day* amusingly draws its viewers into a world in which TV weatherman Phil Connors relives a seemingly endless string of February 2nds, and, given that endless succession of days, develops an amazing number of skills — pianist, ice sculptor, French speaker. A viewer may at first suppose that Phil finds meaning in his seemingly endless life because he never runs out of things or projects that engage his effort and interest. But we should notice that the remarkable expansion of Phil's interests and abilities is actually grounded in one aspect of his character that remains unchanged — his desire to win the love of Rita, the producer of the news show on which he appears. His self remains focused, and the question about the possibility of indefinitely continued growth becomes, therefore, the question whether Rita is an object

13. Taliaferro, "Why We Need Immortality," p. 369.

of love so all-engrossing as to make possible the infinite expansion of Phil's interests.

A fundamental premise of Williams's argument that immortality would necessarily be tedious is his belief that there is no such object; and, of course, this is far from a metaphysically neutral belief. "Nothing less will do for eternity," he writes, "than something that makes boredom *unthinkable*. What could that be? Something that could be guaranteed to be at every moment utterly absorbing? But if a man has and retains a character, there is no reason to suppose that there is anything that could be that."[14] Before we are done, we will have to contemplate the possibility that Williams here rejects.

⌛ ⌛ ⌛

If an endlessly prolonged existence might have, as Christine Overall puts it, the feel of "severe insomnia, in which, having been awake for seemingly endless hours without respite, one feels tired of being aware and exhausted by being oneself and wants only the nothingness of unconsciousness that is afforded, temporarily, by sleep,"[15] it may be that the problem it poses for us would be better described as exhaustion than as boredom. That offers a related but slightly different spin to the idea that the finitude of our capacities gives each person's life a distinct character.

This approach, argued in careful detail by Overall, suggests that a person physically enabled to live forever would — if truly human — still be limited in various ways and, in particular, limited in brain capacity. Therefore, at some point in his endless existence he might well have used to the full all the capacities his brain and body had to offer. "Because of the body's finitude, the body's constancy, so to speak, the immortal would eventually exhaust the capacities to do, to learn, and to experience new things that were within the scope of his particular body. Although the repetition of old familiar activities

14. Williams, "The Makropulos Case," p. 95.
15. Overall, *Aging, Death and Human Longevity*, p. 143.

would still be possible for the immortal, the problem is that even if he had extraordinary abilities and intelligence, every activity he undertook would eventually be 'used up.' "[16]

From this perspective, the problem of a never-ending human life is not best described as boredom, since, after all, repeated activities and experiences of interest would still be possible. The problem is simply that they are endlessly *repeated* activities and experiences. No room remains for growth and development.

Is this really a problem? Here again, I suspect, we can see how any discussion of the desirability of an endless human existence is embedded from the outset in normative claims about what is or is not truly desirable. For example, Overall reports with favor — but to my horror — how "many elderly people with whom I have discussed the longevity issue emphasize that one of the extraordinary gifts of their years after retirement is the opportunity to learn a variety of new things." The point of living longer for them is to become "more than we've ever been before" — to continue to grow.[17] To which I can only say that if I thought the price of retirement were that I had to continue to grow in countless new ways, I would simply keep on grading student papers and forego the Social Security checks.

We need an argument to show that endless growth, constant new achievements and accomplishments, is more desirable than regular repetition of certain enjoyable experiences. This does not mean, of course, that endless repetition of enjoyable experiences is sufficient to satisfy the human heart; it means only that for some of us it may be more attractive than an endless treadmill of accomplishment. But whether we prefer the image of continued growth or that of endless repetition of enjoyable experiences, Overall is right to discern a deep problem here — a problem that she calls an "axiological double bind."

It arises quite naturally. Perhaps some of us are attracted by the idea of endless growth and accomplishment. Perhaps others of us

---

16. Overall, *Aging, Death and Human Longevity,* p. 166.
17. Overall, *Aging, Death and Human Longevity,* p. 45.

think we could endlessly enjoy certain repeated experiences. Or perhaps some of us, focusing less on ourselves, might simply believe that the virtue of love (which says to the loved one, "It's good that you exist") provides a sufficient reason for continuing to live. In any or all of these circumstances, we seem on our way to aiming at a kind of immortality. If a point need never come at which we would feel we had used up life's possibilities for growth, lost the capacity for enjoyment, or wearied of love, we seem committed to the value of an indefinitely extended human life. Yet, continual growth or indefinitely repeated experience seems incompatible with the picture of life as having stages, or as like a meal with a fixed order of courses, which moves through its trajectory to, at some point, its end. Thus, Overall argues, an immortal life may not seem "to be a recognizably human life" — and we find ourselves in that axiological double bind.[18] To live forever, not to be constrained by the limits of finite human bodies, is to be godlike. So if we have good reason to want to live forever, we may be wishing — or striving — to be something other than human beings.

And we are back to the same fork in the road. It could be that human beings are not meant to live forever. Or it could be that we're not meant to live *this kind* of life forever, that part of the point of this life is to draw us on to something still more fulfilling. Either belief would be a way of coming to terms with the axiological double bind.

⚁   ⚁   ⚁

There remains yet a third angle of vision from which we could find reason to wonder whether a distinctively human life should go on forever. Martha Nussbaum has argued at length that many of the virtues we value most get their point precisely from the limits of human life — and, in particular, of course, the limit of mortality. Hence, she suggests, "the removal of all finitude in general, mortal-

18. Overall, *Aging, Death and Human Longevity*, p. 126.

ity in particular, would not so much enable these values to survive eternally as bring about the death of value as we know it."[19]

Greek culture did us the service, she thinks, of carrying out "the thought experiment" of imagining what life would be like for immortals — that is, for the Olympian gods. And the first thing to see about their life, she says, is that "they cannot have the virtue of courage."[20] This impossibility will, she believes, also have implications for other virtues. If I cannot be harmed, I cannot risk everything for someone I love.

While Nussbaum's point is, strictly speaking, true about the Olympians, its reach may be less than we at first suppose. Human beings might, for example, conquer disease and master the aging process and thereby learn how to live an indefinitely extended life — but without becoming invulnerable to enemies. To remain eternally young is not the same as being bullet-proof. Moreover, there are circumstances that do not involve the threat of bodily harm, much less death, but that still require courage. For example, articulating and defending a widely unpopular view, because one believes it to be true, may threaten loss of reputation or friends and require a good bit of courage.

Nussbaum realizes this, of course. She sees that by "reimporting" into a heavenly eternal life pains and disabilities that approach but fall somewhat short of mortality, we may carve out a place even there for virtues such as courage and sacrificial love. "But that is the point: the further mortality is removed, the further they [the virtues] are."[21]

It is indeed the point. And we are reminded yet again that there is no single, metaphysically neutral conception of immortality for us to evaluate. After all, the only conception of heaven, of an everlasting life, in which Christians have any stake is one where the Lamb

---

19. Martha C. Nussbaum, *The Therapy of Desire: Theory and Practice in Hellenistic Ethics* (Princeton: Princeton University Press, 1994), p. 226.

20. Nussbaum, *The Therapy of Desire*, p. 227.

21. Nussbaum, *The Therapy of Desire*, p. 228.

who was *slain* is now enthroned. Perhaps the Olympians, at no risk of being harmed, can have no place for the virtue of courage, but where the Lamb reigns the courage that produced such a heaven is not forgotten but is endlessly honored. We have, therefore, no reason to accept Nussbaum's contention that in heaven there is "no loving friend whose love is such that he risks everything on account of his friend."[22] Quite the opposite, in fact. Mortality, courage, and the love of friends have been "reimported" into this heaven, since the risen Christ still bears bodily the nail prints in his hands. But so has the triumph of the Lamb been reimported. The courage that is no longer needed for battle remains for splendor. And if we insist that, mortality having been overcome, the pathos and nobility of courage cannot really be present in this heaven, what is that but to insist that we would rather honor ourselves as fragile and vulnerable than honor the triumph of the Lamb?

☒　　☒　　☒

What should be evident by now, I hope, is that the desirability of living forever cannot be analyzed in the abstract, apart from the thick webs of belief in which ideas of immortality are embedded. There is no single concept of immortality, and I will therefore take up the question specifically in Christian terms. Christians have thought of the promised eternal life in two somewhat different ways — as a "beatific vision," and as a "new heaven and new earth." From the perspective of these possibilities, boredom could be our fate only in hell.

Bernard Williams had found, we remember, no reason to suppose there could be anything or anyone "that could be guaranteed to be at every moment utterly absorbing." There is, I suppose, no indefeasible argument to persuade us that he is wrong and that, say, Dante's *Paradiso* is right. Nonetheless, if the search is on for

22. Nussbaum, *The Therapy of Desire*, p. 228.

an utterly absorbing object, some may find in Dante's classic depiction of the vision of God a deeper truth than Williams seems able to imagine (or, perhaps, hope for).

If we are made by and for God, then we cannot for a moment understand ourselves — or the other good things of our world — apart from the relation to God. We cannot gain a detached or neutral standpoint from which to see and know ourselves whole. The self that I am is known, finally, only to God — and, hence, in Augustine's famous formula, that self is continually on the way, drawn out of itself, until it rests in God. To care rightly for our own existence is, therefore, impossible apart from that love which says to God, "It's good that you exist."

Every created good that we experience and love may finally fail us, may lack the power to be an utterly — and indefinitely — absorbing object of our love. Perhaps, taken alone and isolated as no created goods should be, they would finally be "used up" and could no longer engage our attention; perhaps, loving them in isolation, we would one day end in boredom. Perhaps, as a character in Wallace Stegner's *The Spectator Bird* puts it, having walked "through the world's great kitchen from end to end," we might then "arrive at the back door hungry."[23]

But the restless heart is not hungry simply for more of the same, for an indefinite prolongation or development of the life we now experience. The delights of this life, even though they are not all-absorbing, are hints that something else — something qualitatively different and not just a quantitative extension of our present experience — is available, even if there is no guarantee that we will find or attain it. The language of "beatific vision" is one way in which Christians have characterized that qualitatively different existence whose goodness can never be exhausted.

One who has been drawn through Christ into the mutual giving and receiving in love that constitutes God's life will have found the

---

23. Wallace Stegner, *The Spectator Bird* (Garden City, NY: Doubleday & Company, 1976), p. 69.

face of beauty — that utterly absorbing face — of which all other beauties are intimations. "There," as Augustine writes, "we shall be still and see; we shall see and we shall love; we shall love and we shall praise."[24] The inclination to adore, which is inscribed in our very being, will have found its proper object. And, as Carol Zaleski suggests, "adoration cannot be boring, for one is gazing at the face of the beloved, and the face of the beloved is inexhaustible."[25] A love of adoration that would be misguided and idolatrous if directed toward any other face here finds the One it has been seeking. Williams is right to suggest that a human being will have a distinct and limited character, which he then takes to mean that the attention of such a distinct person could not be indefinitely captured without tedium by anything or anyone. *Unless,* we might respond, unless one feature of that distinctively human character is that we are created to enjoy the presence of God and cannot be adequately characterized apart from that end.

We should, though, be clear about one important point: The restless heart longs to live forever because it longs for God — not vice versa. To live an indefinitely prolonged life but never to see God, to be always on the way but with no *telos* that gives a point to the journey, might be pleasant in many ways, but it could not satisfy the heart's deepest desire. Perhaps, of course, nothing can. Perhaps Christians deceive themselves, and there is only the journey and our attempts to prolong it and keep it interesting and engaging.

If so, our options will be clear. We may pursue an indefinitely prolonged (but, in the technical sense, "pointless") life, with its possibilities for love and delight. Or we may prefer a life whose limits give it shape and form, like a banquet of many courses that must — precisely in order to be the good thing it is — come to an

---

24. Augustine, *City of God,* trans. Henry Bettenson (New York: Penguin, 1984), 22.30.
25. Carol G. Zaleski, "In Defense of Immortality," in *The Fountain of Youth: Cultural, Scientific, and Ethical Perspectives on a Biomedical Goal,* ed. Stephen G. Post and Robert H. Binstock (Oxford: Oxford University Press, 2004), p. 125.

end. Were those our only alternatives, we might be hard pressed to say which is more to be desired.

And, of course, even if Christians do not deceive themselves, it is possible to say no to the beatific vision: to decline the call of the restless heart and prefer an indefinite prolongation of life as we know it or a limited life whose trajectory moves ineluctably through decline to death. One need not adore — need not be still and see, see and love, love and praise. We have already noted how Nussbaum seems to prefer heroic virtue in the face of vulnerability to the vision of a God who has taken that vulnerability into his own life, overcoming and transforming it. Although she sees this as an affirmation of human bonds of love and friendship, if those bonds cannot be fully and properly human unless brought into relation with God and thereby transformed, hers becomes a prescription not so much for acceptance of vulnerability as for heroic defiance of reality and a refusal to love human beings in the truth of their created reality.

From a rather different angle, the philosopher Jay F. Rosenberg, analyzing Williams's arguments, comments at one point: "It has always struck me that most traditional conceptions of Heaven are notoriously vague about what one who was (ostensibly) fortunate enough to *get* there would actually be *doing* there. They seem to posit that one's 'eternal reward' would consist in just *being* there, 'in God's presence.' But to judge by received accounts, God wouldn't even be an interesting conversational partner."[26] Passing by the flippancy, which will have to find one day its own answer, the charge of vagueness is understandable as an initial reaction, but not as a considered one. Whatever we may say about Williams's belief that boredom must eventually result, even our ordinary earthly loves are often so absorbing and engaging that we eagerly desire "more time" for them. Adam, in Shaw's "Metabiological Pentateuch," did not want to live forever, but he did settle upon the nice round figure of one thousand years. If our ordinary human loves are so engaging,

26. Jay F. Rosenberg, "Reassessing Immortality: The Makropulos Case Revisited." Online at http://www.unc.edu/~jfr/RI-TMCR1.htm. Accessed November 18, 2010.

it is far from clear why God should not be an infinitely interesting conversation partner, even if the chumminess of the image does not capture very well what the experience would actually be like.

☒ ☒ ☒

The language of beatific vision — of endlessly fascinating attention to the presence of a loved one — is not the only way Christians have spoken of what it would mean to live forever with God. They have also spoken of — and hoped for — a "new creation" and a resurrection of the body, though a body that rides time and is not ridden by it. Of course, Christians do not exactly offer an argument for the possibility or likelihood of this. They simply believe it has already once happened. Thus C. S. Lewis recounts "the hardest boiled of all the atheists I ever knew" once saying to him, " 'All that stuff of Frazer's about the Dying God. Rum thing. It almost looks as if it had really happened once.' "[27]

The risen Jesus becomes the promise — a kind of down payment — that the new creation will come in God's good time. As Georges Florovsky, the great Eastern Orthodox theologian, wrote, "From henceforth [that is, after the resurrection of Jesus] every disembodiment is temporary."[28]

It is not easy to picture a life that is both endless and endlessly appealing. (Very probably fewer readers have been captivated by the *Paradiso* than by the *Inferno* or the *Purgatorio*.) Among the most engaging depictions of such an endless life is *The Last Battle,* seventh and last of C. S. Lewis's Chronicles of Narnia. Readers — both children and adults — who have made their way through the first six of the Chronicles are likely to have learned to love Narnia as much as do the children who have been drawn out of our world

27. C. S. Lewis, *Surprised by Joy* (New York: Harcourt, Brace & World, Inc., 1955), pp. 223-24.

28. Georges Florovsky, "The Resurrection of Life," *Harvard Divinity School Bulletin* 17 (1951-52): 18.

into Narnian history. When Narnia is under mortal attack, as it is in *The Last Battle,* they may want to echo words Jill speaks to Jewel, the Unicorn. " 'Oh Jewel — wouldn't it be lovely if Narnia just went on and on — like what you said it has been?' "[29]

In response Jewel does not, like Bernard Williams, argue that it would be boring to live forever; but, still, he knows better than simply to endorse Jill's understandable desire. " 'Nay, sister,' answered Jewel, 'all worlds draw to an end; except Aslan's own country.' " And when night falls on Narnia and the children and Narnians are driven through the stable door, they find themselves in a world of sunlight and color, mountains and waterfalls — a world in which everything that was good and beautiful in Narnia seems somehow to have survived and to be even "more real" than it had been in Narnia itself. They are, in fact, in Aslan's world. "It is," Lewis writes,

> as hard to explain how this sunlit land was different from the old Narnia, as it would be to tell you how the fruits of that country taste. Perhaps you will get some idea of it, if you think like this. You may have been in a room in which there was a window that looked out on a lovely bay of the sea or a green valley that wound away among mountains. And in the wall of that room opposite to the window there may have been a looking glass. And as you turned away from the window you suddenly caught sight of that sea or that valley, all over again, in the looking glass. And the sea in the mirror, or the valley in the mirror, were in one sense just the same as the real ones: yet at the same time they were somehow different — deeper, more wonderful, more like places in a story: in a story you never heard but very much want to know. The difference between the old Narnia and the new Narnia was like that. The new one was a deeper country: every rock and flower and blade of grass looked as if it meant more.[30]

And Jewel, stamping his hoof on the ground, cries out the Augustinian truth: " 'This is the land I have been looking for all my life,

---

29. C. S. Lewis, *The Last Battle* (New York: Macmillan, 1956), p. 84.
30. Lewis, *The Last Battle,* p. 162.

though I never knew it till now. The reason why we loved the old Narnia is that it sometimes looked a little like this.' "[31]

The rallying cry in that world — the rallying cry of the book's last chapters — is "further up and further in." The children and the Narnians go running through winding valleys and up steep hills — up waterfalls, even — meeting countless characters from the earlier stories, many of whom they have known only as almost legendary figures. This new world is, Mr. Tumnus the Faun tells them, " 'like an onion: except that as you continue to go in and in, each circle is larger than the last.' "[32] At the heart of this endlessly expanding world is, of course, Aslan himself, drawing them into a story "which goes on for ever: in which every chapter is better than the one before."[33]

Of course, there are mysteries here, and there is no hope of understanding them or feeling their force unless we are prepared to meet them halfway. The idea of a risen human body, which rides time and is not ridden by it, is surely strange. Yet, as the philosopher Stephen Clark notes in his reflections on science fiction and philosophy, "resurrected beings are not 'the same' because they have 'the same body': their bodies are the same because *they* are."[34] And they *are* only because their existence — and resurrected existence — is God's handiwork.

When week after week throughout the world Christians confess (in the words of the Apostles' Creed) their belief in "the resurrection of the body and the life everlasting," it is strange to suppose we should talk in the abstract about whether a never-ending life would be tedious or would be less desirable than one in which we remained vulnerable, as if there were some neutral conception of such a life on which all agree. There is not. Any conception of immortality worth exploring must be embedded within a larger and

31. Lewis, *The Last Battle*, p. 171.
32. Lewis, *The Last Battle*, p. 171.
33. Lewis, *The Last Battle*, p. 174.
34. Stephen R. L. Clark, *How to Live Forever: Science Fiction and Philosophy* (London and New York: Routledge, 1995), p. 116.

richer context of belief and practice. "We live," as Stephen Clark writes, "between uncomprehended immensities, at the mercy of whatever powers stalk the night. Theists may believe, by faith, that there is a light beyond the darkness. At least that faith makes sense. The mere conviction that the darkness is itself bright day makes none at all."[35]

---

35. Clark, *How to Live Forever,* p. 186.

CHAPTER FOUR

A Generative Life

··

[N]or would there be any reason, why any man should desire to have children, or take the care to nourish and instruct them, if they were afterwards to have no other benefit from them, than from other men.

Thomas Hobbes, *Leviathan*

Each of us comes into a world that has been prepared for us by our predecessors. While generosity is appropriate throughout life, it takes on a distinctive character in old age. More and more, one works for a future that others, not oneself, will enjoy.

Edward Collins Vacek, S.J., "Vices and Virtues of Old-age Retirement"

Once we have produced the next generation, or passed the age when we might have done so, nature does not seem to work very hard to keep us alive. Hence, built deep into our biology is a close connection between reproduction and aging. Moreover, as we have already seen, the one method that almost surely works to extend the life span — caloric restriction — exacts a price of reduced fertility or infertility. Here, too, there appears to be a connection between reproduction and life span.

We can, it seems, work to secure our own future, or we can commit ourselves to our children and others of their generation. We may try to avoid this dilemma by taking comfort in the fact that, as evolutionary biologists remind us, to reproduce is to pass on our genes to the next generation and in that sense to survive and be a winner in the game of life. I doubt, though, whether this is the kind of survival for which most of us hope.

I have borrowed the term "generativity" from the work of Erik Erikson, who may rightly be called "the father of all life cycle studies."[1] We have no term especially apt for naming the virtue that makes us ready, even eager, to produce those who will replace us and to sacrifice ourselves on their behalf. "Generativity" will have to do. One might, of course, argue that this willingness is not virtue but, simply, animal instinct, and perhaps to some degree it is. But Thomas Hobbes did not seem to think that a sufficient explanation. He could think of no reason why parents should have or nourish children apart from the benefits they would gain from their offspring, and only in this way could he make sense of the command that children should honor their parents.[2]

Erikson delineates eight stages of the life cycle, in each of which, he believes, a person needs to acquire certain strengths that make possible growth and development. He characterizes generativity, the seventh stage, as "primarily the interest in establishing and guid-

---

1. Marc E. Agronin, M.D., *How We Age* (Philadelphia: De Capo Press, 2011), p. 65.
2. Thomas Hobbes, *Leviathan,* ed. Michael Oakeshott (New York: Collier Books, 1962), pp. 251-52.

ing the next generation."[3] He does regard it as, to some degree, an instinctual power undergirding the various forms of selfless caring that adults undertake. Generativity is more than that, however, for it must be formed and shaped. As he himself notes, the etymological history of the term "virtue" has to do with a kind of strength "by virtue of" which we are enabled to act powerfully and effectively.[4] Thus, when an analyst says that a patient has improved, he has in mind "an increase in the strength and staying power of the patient's concentration on pursuits which are somehow right."[5]

There may, of course, be many ways in which we enact this concern to care for and guide the next generation.[6] Not only reproduction and parental nurture, but also the teaching of needed skills or transmitting of a culture's system of meaning are included in the virtue of generativity. But the most obvious — and perhaps the most demanding — expression of generativity is having and rearing children. Erikson observes on more than one occasion that human beings *need* to teach the next generation, whether through the obvious form of parental nurture or in countless other, less immediate ways. His concept of "cogwheeling" is "the idea that the needs of the young and those of adults interlock, activate one another, and propel each other through the life cycle. One should think of this less as a calculated exchange and more as an intermeshing of gears that are finely tuned to fit one another."[7] Only through such care for the next generation can we avoid self-absorption. "Individuals who do not develop generativity often begin to indulge themselves as if they were their own one and only child."[8]

3. Erik H. Erikson, *Identity and the Life Cycle* (1959; repr. New York and London: W. W. Norton & Co., 1980), p. 103.

4. Erik H. Erikson, *Insight and Responsibility* (New York: W. W. Norton & Company, 1964), p. 113.

5. Erikson, *Insight and Responsibility*, p. 112.

6. Dan P. McAdams, *The Person: An Introduction to the Science of Personality Psychology*, 5th ed. (Hoboken, NJ: John Wiley & Sons, 2009), p. 363.

7. Don Browning, "An Ethical Analysis of Erikson's Concept of Generativity," in *The Generative Society: Caring for Future Generations,* ed. Ed de St. Aubin, Dan P. McAdams, and Tae-Chang Kim (Washington, DC: American Psychological Association, 2004), p. 247.

8. Erikson, *Identity and the Life Cycle*, p. 103.

We should never underestimate just how demanding such care is. It is demanding not only in the obvious claims it makes upon our time, our energy, and our resources; it is also psychologically demanding in that it asks us to expend ourselves generously on behalf of those who will replace us. As Edward Vacek puts it, "More and more, one works for a future that others, not oneself, will enjoy."[9] It is hard to imagine any greater disciplining of — or, perhaps even, attack upon — our tendency toward self-absorption. Our desire to extend and secure our own future is, to some degree, in conflict with our need to teach the next generation and to leave behind us something of worth.

Here, as so often when we think about aging, it becomes clear that the several goods we desire may be unable to coexist. Whatever the gain might be of retarding aging and extending life indefinitely, doing so could undermine the relation between the generations that shapes and defines so much of our life. Consider the following report of a conversation between Johann Wolfgang von Goethe and Johann Eckermann:

> "From the letters I have written in that period," said Goethe, "I can see quite clearly how one has in every age in life certain advantages and disadvantages in comparison with earlier or later years. For instance, in my forties I was about some things as clear and clever as I am today, and in many respects even better; but now in my eighties I have yet some advantages which I would not exchange for the ones I had then."
>
> "While you are saying this," [Eckermann] said, "I envisage the metamorphosis of plants, and I understand very well that one would not like to return from the period of bloom to the time of leafing, nor from the stage of seed and fruit to the time of blossoms."
>
> "Your simile," said Goethe, "catches my meaning perfectly. Take a well-lobed, mature leaf," he went on with a smile, "do you think it would

9. Edward Collins Vacek, S.J., "Vices and Virtues of Old-age Retirement," *Journal of the Society of Christian Ethics* 30, no. 1 (Spring/Summer 2010): 170.

like to go back from its freest unfolding into the oppressive closeness of the cotyledon?"[10]

Perhaps, of course, some of us will consider the trade well worth making. After all, human beings are considerably more complicated organisms than plants are. Like other animals and unlike plants, we are not rooted in place; characterized by perception, desire, and movement, we transcend naturally given limitations to a much greater degree. Still more, the human animal is marked also by a capacity for reflection, a capacity that brings with it creative possibilities for transforming natural limits.[11] However we sort out and rank the several goods at which such a creature might aim, we do need to recognize that they are to some degree incompatible. We cannot have both an indefinitely extended life span and the virtue of generativity, for the whole point of retarding aging is that we do not want to be replaced.

Although scholars include in Erikson's seventh stage the task of "letting go of those people and things that have been generated and cared for,"[12] it is also instructive to note a certain tension between generativity and the inevitable need to disengage somewhat as we age. Aging requires the patience — both with ourselves and with our world — to acknowledge the limits of what we can do for those who come after us and replace us. On the one hand, therefore, we cannot simply grasp for more — and, indefinitely, more — life without risking the manifold ways our lives are enriched by the relation between the generations. But, on the other hand, simply affirming the goodness of the life cycle also seems inadequate. It offers no guarantee, after all, that our generous care for those who succeed

10. Johann P. Eckermann, *Gespräche mit Goethe*, vol. 2. Discussion from April 12, 1829. Cited in Paul W. Pruyser, "Aging: Downward, Upward, or Forward?" in *Toward a Theology of Aging*, ed. Seward Hiltner (New York: Human Sciences Press, 1975), p. 117.

11. See my discussion, drawing on the thought of Hans Jonas, in chapter 2 of *Neither Beast nor God: The Dignity of the Human Person* (New York and London: Encounter Books, 2009).

12. Dan P. McAdams and Regina L. Logan, "What Is Generativity?" in St. Aubin, McAdams, and Kim, eds., *The Generative Society*, p. 16.

us will have any lasting significance. I suspect that the virtue of generativity needs something more than it can itself provide. What generativity needs is a hope that is grounded in more than the relentless continuation of the life cycle.[13] It needs a transcendent ground, the confidence that our care for the next generation will have lasting significance, and that whatever is incomplete in our care will be completed by the God whose very being is truly generative.

⅀   ⅀   ⅀

Biology teaches us that we may have to choose between age-retardation and a generative commitment to the next generation. But biology cannot tell us what to choose or on what basis to choose. Perhaps in an age when there was little we could do to extend the maximum life span, it might have seemed that we could simply read off from our biological nature the importance of the virtue of generativity. That age is fast fleeting, however, and our capacity for technological transformation of human nature will no longer allow us to take for granted an ongoing cycle of generations. Thus, as the philosopher Richard Sherlock puts it, "On the one hand, nature counsels against dramatic increases or changes in life [span], and on the other, our natural attachment to life combined with our natural creativity and inventiveness leads us to pursue and possibly achieve a dramatic increase in our longevity — which we were supposedly counseled against by nature itself."[14]

When nature gives us such mixed messages, it should be no surprise to find that some will prefer an indefinitely extended life to embeddedness within a cycle of generations (and the aging it necessarily entails). This seems to me worth our attention and concern, but others see little cause for worry. Thus, Susan Jacoby character-

---

13. Don S. Browning, "Preface to a Practical Theology of Aging," in Hiltner, ed., *Toward a Theology of Aging*, p. 161.

14. Richard Sherlock, *Nature's End: The Theological Meaning of the New Genetics* (Wilmington, DE: ISI Books, 2010), p. 24.

izes Leon Kass's idea (though it is hardly an idea peculiarly his) that "people would be less likely to have children if the average life span increased significantly" as "[o]ne of Kass's weirder scenarios." She thinks it "odd to suspect that human beings would stop wanting to reproduce simply because they thought they might live to 100 or 120 rather than 80."[15] Over against her intuitions we might set Larry Temkin's view that "speaking for myself, I think it would be terrible if I came to regard my mother or daughter, not so much as a mother or daughter, but as a peer." And Temkin — in a comment that captures nicely the complex relation between life-extension and the virtue of generativity — notes how odd it would be if such long-lived folk did, in fact, continue to reproduce: "I, for one, don't relish the prospect that if only I lived long enough, I might no longer care about, or even remember, my *first* set of children."[16]

Jacoby is, however, relatively unconcerned. "None of the scientists involved in aging research," she writes, "have been talking about delaying puberty — the only imaginable scenario in which either sex or reproduction could be put off, for the vast majority of people, much beyond the fertility window that now extends, roughly, from the mid-teens to the early forties."[17]

"Susan Jacoby," one wants to say, "meet Stanley Shostak, author of *Becoming Immortal.*" Shostak has a plan, or at least a vision, of how we might go about producing immortal human beings by using both cloning and stem cell therapy prenatally. Neither, taken alone, can really provide immortality. Cloning simply replicates an organism but cannot sustain the life of a particular individual indefinitely. And stem cell therapy, while it may rejuvenate an organism, cannot do so forever and simply delays the inevitable denouement. Put them together, however, and Shostak thinks we may be able to produce people who

15. Susan Jacoby, *Never Say Die: The Myth and Marketing of the New Old Age* (New York: Pantheon Books, 2011), p. 255.

16. Larry Temkin, "Is Living Longer Living Better?" in *Enhancing Human Capacities,* ed. Julian Savulescu, Ruud ter Meulen, and Guy Kahane (Malden, MA: Wiley-Blackwell, 2011), p. 363.

17. Jacoby, *Never Say Die,* pp. 255-56.

are equipped with a never-ending supply of embryonic stem cells that can rejuvenate their bodies. The idea is that, as early as possible in embryonic development, we would replace the embryo's germ cells with a cloned blastocyst that would be a permanent generator of embryonic stem cells, a never-ending resource for bodily regeneration.

In biological development as we know it now, individual human beings are mortal; they age and die. But the DNA of their germ cells passes from one generation to the next and is in that way immortal. "From the point of view of biologists," as Shostak puts it, "achieving immortality depends simply on reversing these roles, creating an endless flow in the somatic line at the expense of the germ line."[18] We should be clear about what this means. It means producing people who, in order that they may be effectively immortal, must "be sterile and remain at a preadolescent age forever but otherwise appear and be perfectly normal."[19] I find it hard not to flag the word "otherwise" so casually inserted into that sentence — as if one could be indefinitely preadolescent but, apart from that minor technicality, "perfectly normal."

Still, we understand the point. In human development, as we ordinarily think of it, the aim is to become a sexually mature adult who is capable of producing the next generation — thereby starting the whole process over again. But this is a kind of development that is predicated on the opposite of individual survival. It requires that one generation give way to the next, and it defines maturity in just such terms. Thus, if we want not an endless round of individuals living out the life cycle but, rather, immortal individuals, we must cease to aim at maturity understood in its ordinary sense.

Shostak invites us to see such a shift — "grabbing life" at the prepubescent stage and preserving it there — as desirable.

> This means preserving human beings at a stage before they are completely developed and mature but at which life is full of excitement,

18. Stanley Shostak, *Becoming Immortal* (New York: SUNY Press, 2002), p. 196.
19. Shostak, *Becoming Immortal*, p. 166.

experience, learning, adventure, and, above all, meaning. Imagine a pre-adolescent, at the physiological age of about eleven, living forever! Such individuals would be close to adulthood and capable of living a relatively fulfilling life, enjoying life and contributing their creativity to it, albeit not reproducing. Immortal, these human beings would be forever young, never fully grown or sexually mature, but never aging.[20]

One wonders what a gathering of middle school teachers would have to say about this proposal. To be sure, Shostak does not necessarily suppose that everyone should be immortalized by being permanently juvenilized in this way. But we could, he thinks, at least produce some individuals who, because they did not reproduce, would be well suited to live in a world with limited resources and, because so long-lived, would have the wisdom to deal with problems as they arise. Nevertheless, he also seems to regard a permanently healthy and youthful life as desirable in itself. Such people will be intellectually creative and "in a perpetual learning mode."[21] A world of these immortals "will be filled with intellectual excitement and dedicated to creative enterprise."[22] One wonders, though. If Erikson was right and human beings have a need to care for the next generation, just how fulfilling — how fully human — will such a life be? We might, at any rate, remind ourselves of Goethe's alternative vision, his suggestion that "a well-lobed, mature leaf" would not want "to go back from its freest unfolding into the oppressive closeness of the cotyledon."

Shostak himself sees some of these issues. In fact, he reflects in quite interesting ways on how the experience of time might be changed for immortals produced in the way he envisions. "Instead of 'living by the clock,' time will be immaterial for the immortals. It will be infinitely accessible, neither running down nor running

20. Shostak, *Becoming Immortal*, pp. 163-64.
21. Shostak, *Becoming Immortal*, p. 207.
22. Shostak, *Becoming Immortal*, p. 208.

out." Such immortal creatures will be able to give little sense to a
term such as "lifetime." They will experience many different moments, but these moments "will not be recalled in seriatim, akin
to the passage of time."[23]

Perhaps Shostak exaggerates what the experience of these immortals would be like, but imagine living in such a constant present,
having little experience of past or future. How shall we characterize
such a life? Is it a godlike existence? Is a desire for this the engine
driving this program? Or, since we are thinking of human beings,
should we have in mind a naturalistic analogue of the life of resurrected believers in heaven — minus, of course, any shared object
of their love and praise? If so, then, at the very least, anyone drawn
to such a project of indefinite life extension should not find the
hope of religious believers to be silly or strange. And believers have
the advantage — or so it seems to me — of not supposing that this
transformation could be the product of their own unaided insight
and technical expertise. As in politics, so also in science, hope for a
gift that comes only through divine power is made immanent, the
work of our hands. I am not inclined to call that progress.

Whatever we may think of these metaphysical reflections, the
implication for earthly life as we know it is clear, and Shostak sees
it with clarity. If we wish to eliminate aging, we must also eliminate
sex and reproduction. In a world in which the human life span has
been indefinitely extended, there will be little place for what I have
called the virtue of generativity. For that virtue is grounded in the
succession of generations, in the fact that those whom we generate
are not simply our descendants but also our replacements.

We cannot yet even begin to carry out the program of juvenil-
ization that Shostak envisions; perhaps we never will be able. But,
as I noted earlier, were the day to come when we could, when our
creative power over nature's givens had been developed that far,
nature itself could not teach us whether such an "advance" was to

---

23. Shostak, *Becoming Immortal*, p. 206.

be desired. For, would it really be an advance? Larry Temkin directs our attention to a prayer used on the Jewish Day of Atonement, spoken to comfort those who had lost loved ones, and offering an alternative vision of what is desirable: "If some messenger were to come to us with the offer that death should be overthrown, but with the one inseparable condition that birth should also cease; if the existing generations were given the chance to live forever but on the clear understanding that never again would there be a child or a youth, or a first love, never again new persons with new hopes, new ideas, new achievements; ourselves for always and never any others — could the answer be in doubt?"[24]

Both the succession of generations nourished by the virtue of generativity and the free creativity that seeks to overcome the need for that succession belong to our nature. Embedded by our finitude in time, we seek in our freedom to transcend it. A freedom that knows no limit may, however, begin to look more destructive than creative. That is why the qualitatively different life for which Christian believers have hoped has not been thought to be in any sense simply an extension of this life — or the product of human ingenuity. As the gift of God, a new creation, it means being drawn into the life shared by Father, Son, and Spirit. If we long for something more than an endless succession of generations, that is the condition toward which Christian hope should be directed. In the meantime, perhaps we should be more concerned to produce and nurture the next generation than to extend our own indefinitely.

⌛   ⌛   ⌛

Because nothing is obvious here, however, we might ask ourselves a simple question: Why have children?

Among the most noteworthy answers in our tradition is that given by Diotima to Socrates and recounted in his speech in praise

---

24. Temkin, "Is Living Longer Living Better?" p. 364.

of love in Plato's *Symposium:* Longing for immortality, love desires to
create. The best we mortal creatures can do to perpetuate ourselves,
the closest mortal beings who are not divine can come to immortality, is to ensure "that there will always be a younger generation to
take the place of the old."[25]

Of course, Diotima (and Socrates) finally envision a transformation of this creative impulse from love of bodies (where it is given a
particular location) to philosophical love of the form of all beauty
wherever it appears. Yet, moving as the speech of Socrates is, I doubt
whether this is the right way to account for the desire to have children, for it is far from clear that the self-spending impulse to create
life out of love's embrace is really an attempt at self-perpetuation
or the fruit of our desire for immortality. I suspect that Aristotle,
as always lower to the ground than Plato, comes closer to the truth
when he focuses on the imperatives of our animal nature. "Male
and female must unite for the reproduction of the species — not
from deliberate intention, but from the natural impulse, which exists in animals generally as it also exists in plants, to leave behind
them something of the same nature as themselves."[26] We might
even say that Aristotle here discerns in nature the divine blessing
enunciated in Genesis 1, that plants and animals are to bring forth
each "according to its kind."

To be sure, it is also true that in the Genesis account human reproduction according to its kind is not left simply to animal impulse.
The divine word directed to humankind, "be fruitful and multiply," is
not only blessing but also command. Evidently there is meaning and
significance to be found in human procreation and the succession
of generations to which it gives rise. We might, therefore, set aside
a search for what motivates human beings to reproduce themselves
and ask instead what deeper purposes in human life are served when

25. Plato, *Symposium,* in *The Collected Dialogues of Plato,* ed. Edith Hamilton and
Huntington Cairns (New York: Pantheon Books, 1966), 207d.
26. Aristotle, *The Politics,* trans. Ernest Barker (London, Oxford, New York: Oxford
University Press, 1958), 1252a.

we have children. And when we seek to articulate those purposes, the three kinds of virtue that the Christian tradition has characterized as "theological" — faith, hope, and love — may offer clues.

The faith that it is worthwhile and good to pass life on to the next generation is grounded in a sense of gratitude for our own life. That anything — ourselves included — should exist at all, that there should be something rather than nothing, is a mystery. G. K. Chesterton, remembering an occasion when the sons of his elderly grandfather were criticizing the General Thanksgiving in the prayer book on the ground that many people had little reason to be thankful for their creation, recalled his grandfather's reply: "The old man, who was then so old that he hardly ever spoke at all, said suddenly out of his silence, 'I should thank God for my creation if I knew I was a lost soul.'"[27]

Before the sheer wonder of existence we must simply bend the knee. That bent knee is nicely depicted and evoked in *The Children of Men,* a novel by P. D. James, set in Great Britain in the year 2021. When the story opens, we learn that no children have been born anywhere in the world since 1995. All males have, for reasons unknown, become infertile, and, hence, the gift of life cannot be passed on. P. D. James helps us feel what such a world would be like by presenting it through the eyes of an Oxford historian, Theo Faron. Fascinated with a young woman named Julian, Theo allies himself with a small movement to which she belongs, a revolutionary group aiming to overthrow the dictatorship ruling Britain. But such political means and goals are put to the side when Julian becomes pregnant (by a priest, Luke, who is also a member of their group).

Julian needs to avoid detection until she has given birth, and so they turn to Theo for help. Coming by night to their hiding place, he needs to be convinced that she can actually be carrying a child. Placing his hand on her abdomen, he feels the child kick, and Julian tells him to listen to its heartbeat.

27. G. K. Chesterton, *Autobiography* (London: Hutchinson & Co., 1937), p. 19.

It was easier for him to kneel, so he knelt, unselfconsciously, not thinking of it as a gesture of homage but knowing that it was right that he
should be on his knees. He placed his right arm around her waist and
pressed his ear against her stomach. He couldn't hear the beating heart,
but he could hear and feel the movements of the child, feel its life. He
was swept by a tide of emotion which rose, buffeted and engulfed him
in a turbulent surge of awe, excitement, and terror, then receded, leaving him spent and weak.[28]

Gratitude for the sheer wonder of life, faithfulness to the gift
we have been given, is at the heart of human procreation, and it
is a rather different thing from just hanging on to the gift and at-
tempting to perpetuate our own life indefinitely. Paradoxically, this
may become clearer to us only as we age, only as we are no longer
moved simply by the "natural impulse" to leave behind something
of the same nature as ourselves that Aristotle discerned. Indeed,

> Age is the hour for praise,
> Praise that is joy, praise that is acquiescence,
> Praise that is adoration and gratitude
> For all that has been given and not been given.[29]

Faithfulness to the life we have received, however long or short,
requires that we see gift and grace at the heart of our existence,
that we develop the capacity for praise "for all that has been given
and not been given."

If faithfulness looks to the past, hope looks to the future. When, in
gratitude for the life we have been given, we generate others like ourselves, when we help to nurture and educate them, we are acknowledging and accepting a world that we cannot entirely control or master.
Hence, having and caring for children does something not only for

28. P. D. James, *The Children of Men* (New York: Knopf, 1993), pp. 153-54.
29. John Hall Wheelock, *This Blessed Earth: New and Selected Poems, 1927-1977* (New
York: Charles Scribner's Sons, 1978), p. 53.

those children but also to and for us. It trains us in virtue. There is, we should not forget, a fundamental difference between a desire to reproduce ourselves or produce an heir and a hopeful spirit willing to give birth to those who will one day replace both us and our projects.

This does not mean, of course, that we should be utterly passive before the next generation. The children we produce we also rear, nurture, and civilize. We pass on, as best we can, a way of life that is distinctively human. But if we are looking to the future in hope, we pass it on, not simply on our own authority or as one final attempt at mastery, but with confidence in God's continued commitment to his creation. Our care and nurture of the next generation should be in service of wisdom, not power. Thus, the psalmist writes:

> I will utter dark sayings from of old,
> things that we have heard and known,
>   that our fathers have told us.
> We will not hide them from their children,
>   but tell to the coming generation
> the glorious deeds of the LORD, and his might,
>   and the wonders which he has wrought.
> He established a testimony in Jacob,
>   and appointed a law in Israel,
> which he commanded our fathers
>   to teach to their children;
> that the next generation might know them,
>   the children yet unborn,
> and arise and tell them to their children,
>   so that they should set their hope in God.

(Psalm 78:2-7)

We cannot guarantee our children's future or the future of children more generally. Therefore, it is only with hope in power greater than our own that we can give life as freely as we have received it, that gratitude can give rise to generosity.

Faithfulness looks to the past, hope looks to the future, and love delights in the present — not just in one's own existence but also in the relation between the generations that marks each present moment. Only thus can we be freed from the tendency to grasp the gift of life and keep it for ourselves. The deepest meaning of a gift, after all, is that it should not be grasped too tightly. It should be received and enjoyed, but passed on.

Drawing on the legendary account of how Atalanta lost a race because she was distracted by several golden apples tossed by her suitor, Hippomenes, who was thus able to defeat her and gain her hand, C. S. Lewis pictures the constant exchange that love involves:

> The golden apple of selfhood, thrown among the false gods, became an apple of discord because they scrambled for it. They did not know the first rule of the holy game, which is that every player must by all means touch the ball and then immediately pass it on. To be found with it in your hands is a fault; to cling to it, death. But when it flies to and fro among the players too swift for eye to follow, and the great master Himself leads the revelry, giving Himself eternally to His creatures in the generation, and back to Himself in the sacrifice, of the Word, then indeed the eternal dance "makes heaven drowsy with the harmony."[30]

Lewis here directs our attention to what Christians regard as the deepest ground of love: the mutual self-giving that marks the divine life of Father, Son, and Spirit. Well before scholars such as Marcel Mauss and Lewis Hyde had explored the complexity of gift exchanges, Christians worshiped a God in whom from eternity the Father gives all that he is and has to the Son, and the Son offers that life back to the Father — a giving and receiving that take place in the bond of love, which is their Spirit.

Our aim in life should not, therefore, be simply to perpetuate ours indefinitely. Indeed, to cling to it is death. The first rule of this

---

30. C. S. Lewis, *The Problem of Pain* (London and Glasgow: Fontana Books, 1957), p. 141.

game of life is, enjoying it, to pass it on — to establish a succession of generations. In this way, by a kind of analogy, our life images the divine life even here and now, as, learning the first rule of the holy game, we give way to those who come after us. It turns out that the generative life is the only real alternative to the sort of self-enclosure that makes no room for mutual love and that in fact is death.

Why have children? Why should or need there ever be a generation other than our own generation? Because the generative life, the relation between the generations, is a school of virtue in which we learn grateful faithfulness to the gift of life we have received, generous hopefulness for those to whom we hand on that gift, and the love that freely gives what it has freely received. Shaped and formed in this school, we may come to see in our own lives that "age is the hour for praise."

CHAPTER FIVE

Patience

....

Our stories work best when they have an ending. As we surf the Internet, we're in danger of forgetting this basic truth. With hypertext, endings are irrelevant — because no one ever gets to one. Reading gives way to surfing, a meandering, peripatetic journey through a maze of threads. . . . If Jane Austen could see what her book Pride and Prejudice *has become on the World Wide Web, she would faint dead away. In the first five sentences, there are four invitations to go elsewhere.*

David Shenk, *The End of Patience*

Be patient, therefore, brethren, until the coming of the Lord.

James 5:7

ON HIS WIDELY read blog, known as "Instapundit," Glenn Reynolds
often links to stories reporting on possible advances in scientific
technologies aimed at age-retardation and life-extension. And having linked to such a report, Reynolds regularly then adds his own
very brief comment: "faster, please." His is a kind of impatience with
the psalmist's description of our life as "threescore years and ten,"
or perhaps "by reason of strength fourscore"; for, even if fourscore,
those years "are soon gone, and we fly away" (Ps. 90:10).

To set our modern thirst for indefinitely extended life over
against the psalmist's acceptance of life's limits suggests that
reflection upon patience may be a fruitful angle from which to
consider the project of age-retardation. How might the virtue of
patience guide our thinking? On the one hand, patience seems to
involve a kind of hopeful anticipation that could move us to seek
an indefinitely extended life span. But, on the other hand, patience
also suggests a capacity to persevere and to accept ills that cannot
be avoided, an attitude that is unlikely to move us to Promethean
attempts at extending life. So we might wonder what, if anything,
would be the point of a virtue such as patience if our lives were
extended well beyond that biblical limit of fourscore years. Would
patience still matter — or, perhaps, matter even more? Would we
still need patience and need to cultivate it in ourselves and in others?

To be sure, it is hard to imagine a human life anything like the
one we live for which the virtue of patience would be entirely un-
necessary. If to be human is to be embodied, all our projects and
activities will have to reckon with the kinds of limits that the body
places upon us, limits that keep us from doing whatever we desire
whenever we desire it. If to be human is to be located, to live in a
particular time and place, we can approach our goals and realize
our desires only in piecemeal fashion, one step at a time. And if to
be human is to live within communities of others who are like us,
we will find that companionship necessarily requires patience.[1]

1. Stanley Hauerwas and Charles Pinches, *Christians among the Virtues* (Notre
Dame, IN: University of Notre Dame Press, 1997), pp. 176-77.

"How," David Harned asks, "could we hold the simplest conversation if we were not willing to wait for the other to speak?"[2]

All of this would still be true in a world in which human beings lived much longer than they do now, in which the maximum human life span had been greatly extended. And all of this is true even now in a world in which some among us hope and work for a day when an indefinitely prolonged human life is possible. Nonetheless, it is worth pondering the point of patience in a world of greatly extended life spans, and it is worth wondering what the role of patience can be for those who here and now commit themselves wholeheartedly to the project of indefinite life extension. After all, in our cultural tradition patience once meant chiefly Stoic fortitude and passive endurance — and then later, reshaped by Christian belief and the example of Christ, a less harsh and more hopeful but still submissive response to the will of God.[3] Surely, the accents must be somewhat different in a world that aims at, or achieves, a considerable advance in the human life span.

We can think of indefinitely extended life both as a condition that might one day be achieved and as a project we might now undertake. How would the virtue of patience be relevant to each of these?

⧗　⧗　⧗

"A being in unending time would be centrifugal," Karl Barth writes.[4] Such a self, constantly moving away from its center, would, no doubt, have countless opportunities to explore and projects to pursue. Were our lives centrifugal in this sense, busyness might be their leitmotif; constant progress and betterment of the human condition might be their aim. Pursuing these opportunities would take time, and

---

2. David Baily Harned, *Patience: How We Wait upon the World* (Cambridge, MA: Cowley Publications, 1997), p. 14.

3. Gerald J. Schiffhorst, "Some Prolegomena for the Study of Patience, 1480-1680," in *The Triumph of Patience: Medieval and Renaissance Studies,* ed. Gerald J. Schiffhorst (Orlando: University Presses of Florida, 1978), pp. 7-9.

4. Karl Barth, *Church Dogmatics,* III/2 (Edinburgh: T. & T. Clark, 1960), p. 565.

successful completion of our projects would be unlikely without at
least some semblance of patience, which would be instrumentally
necessary for such success.

Nevertheless, buried in the deeper reaches of this centrifugal
self would be a kind of impatience, which Søren Kierkegaard, using
an analogy from farming, characterizes in terms of "the rotation
method."[5] One way continually to produce a good yield is constantly
to change fields — what Kierkegaard calls the "extensive" method
of rotation. As an image for life more generally, it suggests constant movement, constant change, "endless journeyings from star
to star," erotic attractions without the fidelity of marriage. "This
method defeats itself; it is plain endlessness." It needs patience
instrumentally, as an aid in the pursuit of one goal or another, but
it is fundamentally restless, going nowhere in particular.

The alternative is an "intensive" method of rotation — in which,
we might say, one goes deeper rather than farther. As the farmer
limited to one field must creatively change crops and modes of
cultivation, so a Don Juan who marries must abandon his desire for
novelty and learn how commitment to one woman can constantly renew love. "The more you limit yourself, the more fertile you become
in invention. A prisoner in solitary confinement for life becomes
very inventive, and a spider may furnish him with much entertain-
ment." The intensive method of rotation requires a patience that
cuts more deeply into the self, that marks the inner person and is
not simply a necessary means to one or another end. "What does it
profit a man," Kierkegaard writes in one of his Christian discourses,

> if he goes further and further and it must be said of him: he never stops
> going further; when it also must be said of him: there was nothing
> that made him pause? For pausing is not a sluggish repose. Pausing is

5. Søren Kierkegaard, *Either/Or,* trans. David F. Swenson and Lillian Marvin Swenson
with revisions by Howard A. Johnson (Garden City, NY: Doubleday Anchor, 1959), pp. 279-
96. For the sake of simplicity I have attributed this view to Kierkegaard. More technically,
it is expressed in the papers of "A," edited by Victor Eremita.

also movement. It is the inward movement of the heart. To pause is to deepen oneself in awareness. But merely going further is to go straight in the direction of superficiality.[6]

Although I will suggest that the restless, extensive method of rotation gives rise to a life that is finally misdirected, we should not fail to give it its due. Even if a kind of impatience and an inability simply to enjoy what is given characterize those who seek to extend life — and extend it more and more — perhaps we should be somewhat more positive about them than Kierkegaard is. They are not simply, as he tends to suggest, bored with life. And because they are not, they remain human. "The devil, above all else, is bored," writes William F. May.[7] He notes that for medieval moralists the vice of sloth — with its complete indifference to created goods and the drying up of desire — was "the most terrifying of sins."[8] Desire, even when misdirected, even when not rightly ordered toward God, nonetheless acknowledges the neediness that is the mark of the creature. For someone who still desires any created good we may have hope; caring for something outside himself, he may learn to wait patiently upon Goodness itself.

The defect of the extensive method of rotation is not chiefly the danger of boredom. It would still offer plenty of occasions for joy. The danger is not so much boredom as meaninglessness, for such a life has no goal other than simple continuance. And to travel through life in that condition is better described as wandering than as journeying. Without a goal, without a home that we are seeking, it becomes harder to explain the point of going on. This is not a matter simply of getting lost now and then while on the way. Man, as G. K. Chesterton once put it, "has always lost his way; but now he has lost his address."[9]

6. Søren Kierkegaard, *Purity of Heart Is to Will One Thing,* trans. Douglas V. Steere (New York: Harper Torchbooks, 1956), pp. 217-18.

7. William F. May, *A Catalogue of Sins* (New York, Chicago, San Francisco: Holt, Rinehart and Winston, 1967), p. 201.

8. May, *A Catalogue of Sins,* p. 195.

9. G. K. Chesterton, *What's Wrong with the World,* in *The Collected Works of G. K. Chesterton,* vol. 4 (San Francisco: Ignatius Press, 1987), p. 77.

Hence, the only patience that would have a place within a centrifugal life of endless opportunity would be entirely instrumental, a necessary means to one or another end. However important that sort of patience undoubtedly is on many occasions, it does not require a centered self. As David Shenk notes in his reflections on the world of hypertext that we now inhabit, a life's story that moves toward no ending can only meander — or surf, as we say.[10] Going nowhere in particular, the self lacks any center other than the desire for still more life; yet life, however long, can never be more than (as Barth puts it) "a fragment which cries out for continuation."[11]

Thus, as long as our life is extended (however indefinitely) in time, patience as an instrumental virtue will be needed. It suits our nature, marked, as it is, by temporality. But human life is also ecstatic. Human desire reaches out beyond created, temporal goods toward "home," toward a condition that cannot be characterized simply in terms of ever new and expanding opportunities — that requires an intensive, not just an extensive, method of rotation. "There is," as Barth says, "no god called Chronos."[12] Hence, we need and seek "the reality of duration and fulfillment, . . . which consists in the perfection of the relationship to God and fellowman."[13] This asks of us a patience that is not instrumental but (we might say) embedded. It requires a willingness to wait upon the universe, or, better, upon God.

Patience that is needed simply to gain something we want is no longer necessary when the desired object has been attained. Of course, there will be other desired things — an endless array — and patience will be needed as we grasp for each in turn. But in each case it will be true that, the object of desire having been attained, patience ceases to be relevant. If, however, the human person is

10. David Shenk, *The End of Patience: Cautionary Notes on the Information Revolution* (Bloomington: Indiana University Press, 1999).

11. Barth, *Church Dogmatics*, III/2, p. 456.

12. Barth, *Church Dogmatics*, III/2, p. 589.

13. Barth, *Church Dogmatics*, III/2, p. 561.

ecstatic — if, as Kierkegaard puts it, the soul does not possess itself — what we really need to gain is not something external, but our own selves. And the patience that gains the self is not instrumental. Its "first requirement" is that we understand that we do not possess ourselves.[14] In waiting upon God, which Kierkegaard called "patience in expectancy," the person in whose soul patience has been embedded is already at the desired goal.[15] Whereas instrumental patience awaits what *may* happen and is therefore at the mercy of time, an embedded patience awaits, as Kierkegaard puts it, what *must* happen — and what, therefore, can never come too late.

Two important conclusions follow about how we ought to live. First, if we wait upon God, resting in the Eternal, patience is always essential, whether we get what we want or fail to get it, whether we get it quickly or slowly. For patience (that is not merely instrumental) "leaves its expectancy up to God and in this way is always equally close to the fulfillment."[16] Thus, Kierkegaard says of Anna (described in the Gospel of Luke as being "of a great age" when she rejoiced at the presentation of the child Jesus in the temple, Luke 2:36-38) that, while her wait, lasting a lifetime, was not "short," it was "brief."[17] Were patience only instrumental, only important as an aid to pursuing our goals, it would be needed more at some times than at others — more in the pursuit of some ends than of others. But the patience needed by human beings whose lives are not only temporal but also ecstatic is always essential, however long or short life may be.

A second implication follows about how we ought to live. The Good is slow, Kierkegaard says, and we must learn that it "can get on" without us.[18] Our responsibility for producing desired accom-

---

14. Søren Kierkegaard, "To Gain One's Soul in Patience," in *Eighteen Upbuilding Discourses,* ed. Howard V. Hong and Edna H. Hong (Princeton: Princeton University Press, 1992), p. 169.
15. Søren Kierkegaard, "Patience in Expectancy," in Hong and Hong, eds., *Eighteen Upbuilding Discourses,* pp. 205-26.
16. Kierkegaard, "Patience in Expectancy," p. 221.
17. Kierkegaard, "Patience in Expectancy," p. 215.
18. Kierkegaard, *Purity of Heart,* p. 102.

plishments is therefore limited. For attention to means rather than ends is central in a life marked by patience. Once again Kierkegaard comes round to the same point: "He whose means are invariably just as important as the end, never comes too late."[19] Even were the human life span extended far beyond what we now experience, the most fundamental moral conditions of our lives would not be altered. Instrumental patience would be needed, but always qualified and relativized. A person is not "eternally responsible for whether he reaches his goal within this world of time. But without exception, he is eternally responsible for the kind of means he uses. And when he will only use or only uses those means which are genuinely good, then, in the judgment of eternity, he is at the goal."[20]

Suppose, then, that the condition of our life changed, that our maximum life span were extended dramatically. Patience — in its most important moral sense — would be unchanged. Or, on the other hand, suppose we never succeed in the project of age-retardation. Patience — in its most important moral sense — will be unchanged. The length of the life span does not change the nature of virtue — or, at least, of this virtue.

⧗　　　⧗　　　⧗

But what about life-extension not as a condition already achieved but as a project that we undertake here and now? What does the virtue of patience suggest to us about the wisdom of such an undertaking?

In the modern era, and certainly in the twentieth century, impatience marked primarily our political aspirations. Putting a human shoulder to the wheel of history in order to try to do God's work for him, we hoped to fashion, if not a utopia, at least a better world here and now. In the twenty-first century we have focused those impatient hopes of mastery more on science than on politics, and perhaps it will prove less intractable.

19. Kierkegaard, *Purity of Heart*, p. 203.
20. Kierkegaard, *Purity of Heart*, p. 202.

But what if hope for such mastery fundamentally misunderstands who we are? "Patience is," David Harned writes, "simply the embrace of what we are. We are patients, whether we like it or not; we cannot escape our own nature. We come into the world as patients and we leave it as patients, but even in our days of greatest strength our condition is no different."[21] This need not mean simple acquiescence in our present circumstances or the current limits of human life, whatever those may be — as if we were not also agents. It simply means that our agency is always limited, qualified by our more fundamental condition as patients needing patience. This is the lesson William Temple's father tried to teach his son, who, as a relatively young man, impatient to be accomplishing his goals, complained of lack of time to get done what needed doing. "William," said his father, "you have all the time there is."[22] That is to say, all the time there is for one who is not wandering but journeying, who must learn to wait for "the coming of the Lord." Our agency is not mastery but participation in a power greater than our own.

There is in principle nothing wrong with trying to retard aging and extend human life. But as a human project to which we must always say "faster, please," it may bring with it considerable loss. Three kinds of loss seem especially significant.

First, like Kierkegaard's farmer who practices the extensive method of rotation, we may acknowledge no limit to our desires. How easily we can forget that aiming at retarding aging and extending indefinitely the life we now live is not the only kind of mastery, nor is it the only or most creative display of human agency. The psychologist Paul Baltes noted how, as we grow older, we adapt to our diminishing capacities through three different strategies — selection, optimization, and compensation. Baltes then provided a beautiful illustration of this in a story about Arthur Rubenstein, the virtuoso pianist.

21. Harned, *Patience,* p. 182.
22. Richard John Neuhaus, *As I Lay Dying* (New York: Basic Books, 2002), p. 65.

At 80, Rubenstein was asked how he managed to still give such excellent concerts. Over the course of several interviews, he offered three reasons. First, he played fewer pieces — an example of selection. Second, he practiced these pieces more often — an example of optimization. Finally, he played slow movements more slowly, to make it appear as though he were playing the piano faster in the fast movements than he was actually able to — an example of compensation.[23]

In embracing our status as patients, even and especially in our moments of mastery, we are protected against the ruinous urge to want everything. We are not lured into wanting what Michael Sandel called "a world inhospitable to the unbidden," even the unbidden diminishment of our own skills and capacities.[24] Wanting everything in politics turned the twentieth century in terribly destructive directions from which we have yet to recover. Wanting everything in science and medicine can easily do the same.

As we see ourselves less as patients whose lives are marked by limits, as we suppose ourselves to have ever-increasing responsibility for overcoming those limits, we may lose one of the great blessings of being human — namely, that, as Sandel puts it, "we are not wholly responsible for the way we are."[25] Exercising agency within limits, within boundaries shaped by the virtue of patience, may in the end be the secret to a kind of creativity that does not conceal destructive urges.

Always saying "faster, please" to the project of life-extension may bring a second kind of loss in its wake — namely, a loss of meaning. "Our stories work best when they have an ending," as David Shenk puts it.[26] Without the sense of an ending, it is harder to find significance in every step along the way. When in his *Poet-*

23. Paul B. Baltes, "Facing Our Limits: Human Dignity in the Very Old," *Daedalus* 135, no. 1 (Winter 2006): 35.

24. Michael J. Sandel, *The Case against Perfection* (Cambridge, MA: The Belknap Press of Harvard University Press, 2007), p. 86.

25. Sandel, *The Case against Perfection*, p. 87.

26. Shenk, *The End of Patience*, p. ix.

ics Aristotle famously characterizes a story's plot as a whole having beginning, middle, and end, he compares such a narrative plot to the life of an organism. "To be beautiful, a living creature . . . must not only present a certain order in its arrangement of parts, but also be of a certain definite magnitude."[27] If a creature's size is too vast — "say, 1000 miles long" — we will not, Aristotle thinks, be able to see its wholeness and unity. Just so, a well-constructed story or plot "must be of some length, but of a length to be taken in by the memory."[28] Aristotle does not deny that a truly excellent poet may be able to stretch a plot somewhat beyond its capabilities, but he does not think there are likely to be many whose abilities rival Homer's. A living being is an organic unity, and we may not be able to appreciate and savor the goodness of its life unless that life has a shape that does not extend indefinitely: a shape that is marked by beginning, middle, and, even, end.

I do not wish to underrate the goodness of extended life, nor would I ignore the pleasures each step along the path of longer life may bring. But for these steps to have meaning, for them to give our lives significance, there must be more to them than the overcoming of old limits. They must go somewhere, have some end, find their place in a story whose overall shape makes and gives sense. Without that, it may be hard to know why we should go on at all, and the desire for more life may undercut itself. If we read *Pride and Prejudice* online, and in the process follow links here and there indefinitely, we may be enriched in many ways. But we also suffer a loss of even greater significance, for we lose the point of the story and the satisfaction of its ending.

A third kind of possible loss may be the most important of all. Constantly seeking to overcome the givenness of life, the limits that circumscribe our projects and our time, we may also lose a sense of life's giftedness. It is patience — the virtue that neither grabs nor grasps, that does not simply say "faster, please" — that makes place

27. Aristotle, *Poetics* (New York: The Modern Library, 1954), chapter 6 (p. 233).
28. Aristotle, *Poetics,* chapter 9 (p. 236).

in life for its accompanying virtue, gratitude. For without patience we can receive nothing as a gift, nothing that comes apart from our own effort and achievement.

When the biblical character Job has lost both his wealth and his children, he says: " 'The LORD gave, and the LORD has taken away; blessed by the name of the LORD' " (Job 1:21). Kierkegaard invites us to observe that when Job has suffered the loss of almost everything he holds dear, the first thing he says is that the Lord gave. That is to say, "his heart first expanded in thankfulness."[29] His first impulse was gratitude for the blessings given him and now taken from him. Each blessing had not, Kierkegaard notes, "become less beautiful because it had been taken away."[30]

Of course, someone else — one of us, perhaps — might not respond as did patient Job. Such a person might well react with impatience. "What he once had been able to do, he now wanted to be able to do again."[31] Understandable as such impatience is, it blinds us to the gift we have received, and it makes gratitude impossible.

⌛   ⌛   ⌛

If the effort to extend life indefinitely may diminish life in these three ways, an even greater loss may be our inability to see not just life but also old age in particular as a gift — a blessing that not only requires patience of us but, more significantly, offers the opportunity for patience.

In the *Republic* Plato pictures Socrates talking to the aged Cephalus and asking him to tell them what it is like to be at that point along the road of life. Cephalus grants that some older people lament their condition, believing that the best things have now been taken from them, but he does not agree. Rather, he finds in old age "a great

29. Søren Kierkegaard, "The Lord Gave, and the Lord Took Away; Blessed Be the Name of the Lord," in Hong and Hong, eds., *Eighteen Upbuilding Discourses*, p. 115.
30. Kierkegaard, "The Lord Gave . . . ," p. 116.
31. Kierkegaard, "The Lord Gave . . . ," p. 117.

tranquility" when "we are rid of many and mad masters."[32] Among
those mad masters may be the thirst for longer life. To be drawing
near the end of life can, at least for some, be liberating. It frees us
from the tyranny of accomplishment, teaching us that "real freedom comes at the end of a process rather than at the beginning."[33]

Without supposing that old age is always tranquil or that everyone will experience it as blessing, we should nonetheless remember
that it may, as Cephalus noted, offer the great gift of a time for patience and freedom from hurry. That, at any rate, was the testimony
of the Quaker philosopher D. Elton Trueblood, who as himself a
man past 80 years of age noted what he called a "paradox" of the
experience of time in old age: "that we can be vividly conscious
of our inevitable temporal finitude and yet enjoy its abundance,
because we are in no great hurry."[34] Because, that is, we have been
given time for patience, because we have all the time there is.

32. Plato, *Republic,* in *The Collected Dialogues of Plato,* ed. Edith Hamilton and Huntington Cairns (New York: Pantheon Books, 1966), 329c.
33. D. Elton Trueblood, "The Blessings of Maturity," in *The Courage to Grow Old,* ed.
Philip L. Berman (New York: Ballantine Books, 1989), p. 299.
34. Trueblood, "The Blessings of Maturity," p. 297.

CHAPTER SIX

A Complete Life

Western culture has relied on two archetypal images to represent intuitions of the wholeness or unity of life — the division of life into ages (or stages) and the metaphor of life as a journey.

Thomas Cole, *The Journey of Life*

The true cure for death . . . cannot lead simply to an indefinite prolongation of this current life. . . . It would need to create a new life within us, truly fit for eternity.

Pope Benedict XVI, "Baptism as the Beginning of a Process"

An earlier version of this chapter appeared as "A Complete Life," in *First Things*, no. 219 (January 2012): 25-31.

JOHN HALL WHEELOCK, a minor twentieth-century poet — dubbed "the last romantic" in the title of his oral autobiography — captured movingly some of the reasons we desire more life, our sense (nevertheless) that a complete human life cannot mean an indefinitely extended one, and the pathos we experience when (as we should) we hold both of these views simultaneously. Here is his poem, "An Ancient Story."

Young thrush, heard singing from some hidden bough
In the west wood nearby,
Your tender song recalls to memory
A day, still unforgotten now,
That blessed day when we,
My dear true love and I,
After such sundering, such salt seas between,
Once more together, in this same west wood
Where we so often had together been,
In silence stood,
Listening to your loved song,
Unchanged through all these many years,
And kissed, while the soft May-time green
Swam round us, prismed in our tears.
Oh, if you will,
Sing to us, now as then,
That self-same song —
We are together still,
Bring back again
That day when all was young.

Or, since this may not be —
When, at a not too far-off time, our time is come,
And, under the cloudy shade
Of some, perhaps, young springtime-flowering tree,
Deep in the earth our bodies shall be laid,

Oh, from a hidden bough,
Let fall upon us, where we lie at rest,
Together still, your antique elegy,
The half-remembered story
Of two fond lovers, faithful to their vow,
For love's sake, doubly blest;
Pour out, pour out, upon that quiet air
The pent-up fury and ardor in your breast,
Shatter the silence there
With love's high plaint amid things transitory —
Oh, if you will,
Sing to us — then as now
Together still —
That self-same song,
Life's fierce and tender glory
Once ours, when all was young.[1]

Although my train of thought here is moving, however slowly and deliberately, in a Christian direction, this poem with which I begin is, I think, essentially pagan. That does not make it any less moving, nor is that a way of saying it is simply misguided. As C. S. Lewis once put it, "a Pagan . . . is a man eminently convertible to Christianity. He is essentially the pre-Christian, or sub-Christian, religious man. The post-Christian man of our day differs from him as much as a *divorcée* differs from a virgin."[2] Christian humanists have always known that there may be much to learn about our shared humanity from those who are not Christians. They may often help us to see more fully and think more clearly, even if we cannot rest entirely content with what may be known apart from Christ.

"An Ancient Story" expresses the understandable hope of lovers

1. John Hall Wheelock, "An Ancient Story," *The Sewanee Review* 81 (January-March 1973): 73-74.
2. C. S. Lewis, *God in the Dock: Essays on Theology and Ethics* (Grand Rapids: Eerdmans, 1970), p. 172.

for more time together. "Sing to us, now as then, / That self-same song." It seems both natural and right that they should desire this. Nevertheless, even if the song of the thrush may be "Unchanged through all these many years," they — and we — are not. However much we might long to "Bring back again / That day when all was young," this "may not be." When the lovers are finally and unchangingly "Together still," it will be because deep in the earth their bodies have been laid. And the song of the thrush, then, will be "love's high plaint amid things transitory" — love's grasping for something more in a world that cannot, finally, "Bring back again / That day when all was young."

Quite naturally we long for more life — for an indefinitely extended life — and yet this may not be. How, therefore, shall we think of the human being? As a vain and futile animal, doomed to discontent and unable to flourish — for whom life cannot offer a satisfying completion? As one who, even "amid things transitory," can attain what we might call a complete life that has a kind of integrity and wholeness, all its threads gathered up into a meaningful unity? Or, to look from yet a third angle, might there be a way, without thinking of human life as vain and futile, to acknowledge and make sense of its incompleteness?

Thomas Cole, historian of aging, observes that our attempts to picture a complete life have relied primarily on two images: life as a series of ages, and life as a journey.[3] While not entirely dissimilar, these two images invite us to think of life's wholeness in somewhat different ways.

☒   ☒   ☒

Among the most famous descriptions of life's stages is that given by Aristotle in Book II of his *Art of Rhetoric*. The subject arises there almost by accident. Because he thinks that "all men are willing

3. Thomas R. Cole, *The Journey of Life: A Cultural History of Aging in America* (Cambridge: Cambridge University Press, 1992), p. xxx.

to listen to speeches which harmonize with their own character,"
Aristotle suggests that a student of rhetoric must consider how
different listeners will respond to speeches they hear.[4] Hence, we
need to understand the ages of life if we are to speak in ways that
will appeal to different sorts of hearers.

Aristotle distinguishes three stages — youth, the prime of life,
and old age — comparing and contrasting them with respect to
various aspects of behavior. Thus, for example, while the young
prefer what is noble to what is useful, those who are old become
cautious, preferring what they find useful. The young, not yet having
experienced many failures (or so Aristotle supposes), are hopeful
and optimistic; the elderly, whose experiences indicate that "all
events generally turn out for the worse," tend "to live in memory
rather than in hope." In contrast to the young, who "think they
know everything, and confidently affirm it," the old are constantly
adding a "maybe" or a "perhaps" to all that they say.[5]

We get the picture. Aristotle has a rather jaundiced view of old
age, and he may underestimate the disappointments and problems
characteristic of youth. But, rightly or wrongly, he tends to think of
the young as passionate, impulsive, and ambitious — characterized
by excess of many kinds. The old are also marked, though in their
own peculiar way, by excess. They are characterized, as Aristotle's
unusual formulation puts it, by "an excessive lack of energy."[6]

Perhaps surprisingly, Aristotle actually has far less to say about the
prime of life. In terms of physical strength and health, he places that
prime — disconcertingly for many of us — at ages thirty to thirty-five.
The mind, he says, reaches its prime around forty-nine years of age.
The reason he says relatively little about the prime of life becomes
clear to the reader. Depicting both youth and old age as excessive in
their different ways, he thinks of the prime of life as a kind of mean

4. Aristotle, *The "Art" of Rhetoric,* trans. John Henry Freese (London: William Heine-
mann; New York: G. P. Putnam's Sons, 1926), 2.13.

5. Aristotle, *Rhetoric* 2.13.

6. Aristotle, *Rhetoric* 2.13.

between these two extremes. "It is evident," he writes, "that the character of those in the prime of life will be the mean between that of the other two, if the excess in each case be removed."[7] The conduct of those in life's prime will be guided by neither the noble alone nor the useful alone, but by both at once. They face the future with both courage and self-control. They are neither overconfident nor too hesitant, seeking to judge in accord with the facts before them.

This middle stage is life's pinnacle, and in relation to it the other two stages constitute either preparation or decline. The complete life has a rounded shape, a trajectory, but its stages of preparation and decline take their significance primarily from that prime of life when we are at the peak of our powers and most likely to display the kind of practical wisdom that flows from virtues well established. It is, it seems, this prime of life that shows us what a human being at his best, a truly flourishing man or woman, can be — one whose virtuous actions display the *logos* or reason that distinguishes human beings from the other animals.

As is well known, however, Aristotle has another — probably competing — concept of what makes a human life complete. *Logos* is displayed not only in our doing but also in what we might call our beholding — not only in practical but also in theoretical reason, not only in action but also in contemplation. Having spent the bulk of his *Nicomachean Ethics* examining how practical wisdom takes shape in lives of virtuous doing, in its tenth and final book Aristotle describes that active life as flourishing only in "a secondary sense."[8]

The most complete human life is enacted not in doing but in beholding, in *theoria,* an entirely self-contained activity of the mind. It attempts neither to make nor to accomplish anything, having no further goal beyond the beholding itself. It is, as the philosopher Kathleen Wilkes writes, rather like seeing: "attainment is predicated at the same time as the activity: means and

7. Aristotle, *Rhetoric* 2.14.
8. Aristotle, *Nicomachean Ethics,* trans. Martin Ostwald (Indianapolis: Bobbs-Merrill, 1962), 1178a9.

ends coalesce."[9] We have come to call it "contemplation," from the Latin translation of the Greek *theoria*. Josef Pieper reminds us that "when Anaxagoras was asked, 'To what end are you in the world?' he answered: *'Eis theorian* — in order to behold the sun, moon, and sky' "[10] — a sentiment that bears at least a certain kinship to the famous answer to the first question in the *Westminster Catechism,* "What is the chief end of man?" Answer: "To glorify God and to enjoy him forever." Such beholding is unlike our doing in that it aims at no accomplishment. Nevertheless, as Pieper has written, it "emphatically involves interest, participation, attention, purposiveness."[11] It is by no means passive.

The exercise of theoretical reason in beholding has a timeless quality, for its objects must be, as Amélie Oksenberg Rorty notes, "necessary, unchanging, eternal, self-contained, and noble."[12] It thus freely transcends the limits of life's normal course. The activity of contemplation is complete in itself and offers, therefore, an image of human flourishing different from a picture of life as composed of stages that, taken together, make for a complete life. And Aristotle himself seems uncertain how to hold together or assess the relation between these two different depictions of a complete life. The life of *theoria,* though it is an activity of what is highest in us, may seem to soar so far above the needs and activities of what he calls "our composite nature" as to be almost "more than human."[13] "It is because he is not sure who we are," Thomas Nagel tellingly writes, "that Aristotle finds it so difficult to say unequivocally in what our eudaimonia [our flourishing] consists."[14]

9. Kathleen V. Wilkes, "The Good Man and the Good for Man in Aristotle's Ethics," in *Essays on Aristotle's Ethics,* ed. Amélie Oksenberg Rorty (Berkeley: University of California Press, 1980), p. 350.

10. Josef Pieper, *Happiness and Contemplation* (South Bend, IN: St. Augustine's Press, 1998), p. 99.

11. Pieper, *Happiness and Contemplation,* p. 73.

12. Amélie Oksenberg Rorty, "The Place of Contemplation in Aristotle's *Nicomachean Ethics,*" in Rorty, ed., *Essays on Aristotle's Ethics,* p. 379.

13. Aristotle, *Nicomachean Ethics* 1177b26-30.

14. Thomas Nagel, "Aristotle on Eudaimonia," in Rorty, ed., *Essays on Aristotle's Ethics,* p. 8.

In order to know how best to characterize a complete human life, we have to know what sort of being a human being is. Much of what Aristotle has to teach us suggests that the trajectory of a complete life — a fulfilled and flourishing life — will be marked by stages that move from preparation to optimal performance to decline. There is something satisfying about that picture, which is suited to our nature as organic, bodily creatures. It incorporates within it the relation between the generations that cuts so deeply into all our lives and marks us. It includes decline in our image of completion, and, in so doing, prepares us for the day when "Deep in the earth our bodies shall be laid." And yet, Aristotle himself forces us to set a question mark beside this image of completion, leaving us uncertain whether we should really accept it as a satisfactory understanding of a fulfilled and flourishing human life. Whatever may or may not be possible, "love's high plaint amid things transitory" will set itself against any too-easy acquiescence in this image of completion. The wholeness we seek and need may be something that draws us out of ourselves — out of the limitations of life's finite course into an indefinite freedom. That, at least, will be true if, as William F. May has written, "the self turns out to be ecstatic — pitched out beyond itself toward that in which it finds its meaning."[15]

⧗   ⧗   ⧗

In the early modern period of Western history, the idea of a life divided into several general stages or ages took on greater specificity in the concept of the career. Childhood and youth were a time of preparation for one's career, and old age became the time when one was "past one's peak" or "over the hill." A career is something for which one takes personal responsibility, something that requires careful planning. Margaret Urban Walker notes that many phi-

15. William F. May, "The Aged: Their Virtues and Vices," in *The Patient's Ordeal* (Bloomington and Indianapolis: Indiana University Press, 1991), p. 136.

losophers, however different their views may be in other respects, have thought in these terms. Thus, John Rawls thinks of human life as lived according to a rational long-term plan; Bernard Williams describes life's "constitutive projects" that will "carry us into the future with a reason for living"; Charles Taylor suggests that we have failed as persons if our "lives as a whole do not sustain a meaningful narrative." They all share, Walker believes, "the idea of an individual's life as a self-consciously controlled career. It binds a whole life or lifetime together in a unified way for which the individual is accountable. The individual's ability to account for this life — to bring forward its plan, project, or narrative plot — testifies to the individual's *self*-control."[16]

When life is envisioned in this way as a career, retirement becomes an obvious problem, since it seems to bring one's career to a close and is simply a period of decline. Marking the end of significant activity, growth, and development, it becomes entirely unrelated to the previous course of life, which loses its coherence. Hence, we have come to look for ways to incorporate conscious and continued growth and accomplishment into old age — a transposition, but also a continuation, of the active life. One way to attempt this is what Robert Butler called the "life review," an effort to think through and sum up the meaning of one's life and the course it has taken.[17] Butler himself regarded this as a nearly universal tendency of those nearing death, a natural attempt to survey and reintegrate one's past experience.

Similarly, H. R. Moody has described what he terms "conscious aging." This is something other than simply adapting, however successfully, to age-related changes; for adaptation in itself requires no real growth in consciousness or wisdom. Adaptation does not continue to advance the course of one's life. Conscious aging, by

16. Margaret Urban Walker, "Getting Out of Line: Alternatives to Life as a Career," in *Mother Time: Women, Aging, and Ethics* (Lanham: Rowman & Littlefield, 1999), p. 102.

17. R. N. Butler, "The Life Review: An Interpretation of Reminiscence in the Aged," *Psychiatry* 26 (1963): 65-75.

contrast, "typically entails a long struggle" and involves continued active growth, "increasing integration of divergent elements
of the self, both rational and emotional, to yield a more complex
structure."[18]

As with Aristotle's attempt to unravel the relation of active and
contemplative lives, here too we must say that we cannot know
what it means for our lives to flourish unless we know who we are.
And if we are ecstatic beings, pitched out beyond ourselves, any attempt definitively to review our lives or integrate fully their divergent
strands may be futile; for we cannot find a place from which to see
ourselves whole, to catch the heart and hold it still.

That is the profound insight of Book 10 of Augustine's *Confessions*. Even those students who are fortunate enough these days to
be given an opportunity to read the *Confessions* are seldom asked to
go beyond Book 8 — thereby missing the point. For when in Book 10
Augustine begins to take stock of how well he is doing in his attempt,
since his conversion, to live the Christian life, he comes to see that
this is a question he cannot answer. A reader beginning the *Confessions* is likely to get the impression that its author understands
the course of his life, but it turns out that this sort of life review
can be done only by God. Unable to see himself whole and entire,
Augustine finally has to acknowledge that our lives are a mystery
to us. "What then am I, my God? What is my nature? A life various,
manifold, and quite immeasurable. . . . I dive down deep as I can,
and I can find no end."[19] God knows the course of Augustine's life
better than he knows it himself, and, hence, the recounting of that
life must become confession. "I will confess what I know of myself,
and I will also confess what I do not know of myself."[20] We cannot
really determine whether the course of our life, passing through its
various stages, has had the kind of integrity and wholeness needed

18. Harry R. Moody, "Conscious Aging: A New Level of Growth in Later Life." At
http://www.hrmoody.com/art4.html. Accessed February 4, 2011.

19. St. Augustine, *Confessions*, trans. Rex Warner (New York: New American Library,
1963), 10.17.

20. Augustine, *Confessions* 10.5.

to make it complete. The division of life into ages offers a certain sense of completion — but at the cost of our capacity for free self-transcendence, for beholding a beauty that is timeless. And the related vision of life's course as a career offers what is, in the end, only an illusion of self-control and self-understanding.

⚕   ⚕   ⚕

Perhaps the somewhat different image of a journey can give us a unified picture of life — acknowledging that we are finite beings making our way through life's course, but without exaggerating our capacity for control or our ability to know ourselves. To think of life from this angle, I turn from Aristotle to Karl Barth, that great twentieth-century theologian of whom Hans Frei once wrote: "Had he not been a theologian, he would have been more widely recognized as one of the towering minds of the twentieth century."[21]

In volume III/4 of his *Church Dogmatics* Barth discusses the ages or stages of life but sets them into the larger context of vocation, of God's call to individuals.[22] That larger context, it seems, incorporates life's stages into a journey whose end and meaning we cannot entirely discern. How could we, since the call comes from God, who remains free? "We cannot be permitted to anticipate the freedom of God's commanding, and therefore of His controlling of our real vocation, by any science of youth and age, however well-grounded." Acknowledging that divine freedom, we cannot tell anyone precisely how to determine his or her calling. We can characterize in general the kinds of limitations that will prepare us to hear the call, and some of those limitations will be related to our stage in life, but the freedom of God will have a transformative impact on how we think about those stages. For

---

21. Hans W. Frei, *Types of Christian Theology* (New Haven and London: Yale University Press, 1992), p. 148.

22. Karl Barth, *Church Dogmatics,* III/4 (Edinburgh: T. & T. Clark, 1961), pp. 607-18. The quoted passages from Barth in the discussion that follows are all taken from this section of the *Church Dogmatics.*

in any moment we meet the call of God anew, and, hence, in every moment it is as if we were "just setting out."

Having begun with the assertion that we always remain free within our limitations, Barth can then think through those limits — the kinds of limits that characterize the different ages of a person's life. Like Aristotle, he thinks of three such stages, and it will be useful to set some of his characterizations alongside Aristotle's. Each age has, on his account, its special opportunities and responsibilities.

Like Aristotle, Barth, too, sees in the young an orientation toward the future and a certain optimistic energy. The past, because for them it has been relatively short, need not, he says, weigh too heavily upon those who are young. "The thought of impotence in face of a blind fate should be far from" them. Having little experience, they need not be slaves of habit. This depiction — though characteristically Barthian in cadence — is not unlike Aristotle's; yet, it is given a different twist. These characteristics are not weaknesses. They are not an extreme resulting from minimal experience. On the contrary, they provide positive, special opportunities for acting with a "fruitful astonishment." And, indeed, a part of the special responsibility of the young is to provide for the older and the old an example of true youthfulness — a sentiment we can scarcely imagine on the lips of Aristotle.

Every bit as much as Aristotle, Barth realizes that one who is old will have experienced enough to have reason for caution, for knowing how little we can often accomplish. But for Barth this is again an opportunity: "the supremely positive fact that the old man has the extraordinary chance to live" in faith that God has committed himself to our cause. He has "the privilege of living . . . in terms of a verse which he has often sung with gusto: 'With force of arms we nothing can, Full soon were we downridden; But for us fights the proper Man, Whom God Himself hath bidden.' " Hence, the old person need not live as much in memory as Aristotle supposed; for true old age should not be marked by "automatic repetition of earlier answers." No longer imagining, if he ever did, that he goes to meet God on his own terms, it is the old person's "special opportunity" to discover that the initiative always lies with God — and in this discovery to be an example for all who are younger.

The "middle years" of life — not, it is perhaps worth noting, the "prime of life" in Barth's discussion — are not simply a mean between two extremes, though there is a hint of that. Thus, for example, this is the time for us to act with "measured haste" — the time, Barth says, for venture and work by one who now has a certain amount of experience in life but is not so close to the end that he might be exhausted or tempted to resignation. With relatively fewer limitations than mark those at other stages of life, those in the middle years can seize the responsibilities set before them. Their special opportunity is to be an example — both to those who are older and those who are younger — of people "who are truly ripe for obedience."

We can see, then, what Barth has done. On the one hand, he acknowledges that our lives have a relatively clear trajectory, marked by specific stages. Hence, God claims each of us and calls us at particular moments in life's finite course. And if we want to know what God asks of us, that can only mean what he asks of us at the particular point where we find ourselves. Barth's focus, however, is not on the age or stage of development of the person called but on his relation to the One who calls. I am not, Barth says, to take my age as such seriously but, rather, to take myself at my various ages "as the creature of God and object of His providence subject to His judgment."

"The particular seriousness of every age does not consist, therefore, in a special attitude which one has to assume to life in youth, maturity or old age, but in the seriousness with which at every age one has to go from the Lord of life to meet the Lord of life and therefore to try to live as though for the first time or as though this were the only age." Each age of a person's life takes its meaning in part from its relation to other ages, but each age also has its own independent significance. Each is equidistant from the God who calls. Youth and old age, in particular, do not draw their meaning primarily from that middle stage of life when we are at the peak of our powers; they are not primarily characterized as preparation and decline. Each age has its own special opportunities; each serves in its own way as exemplar for the others. A true youthfulness, maturity, and elderliness can mark every age of life.

This means that each person is called by God not simply to progress through fixed stages of life, nor to fashion a career entirely under his or her own control, but to set out on a journey, which — because it is governed by the providence of a God who is always free — must have a course whose ending cannot be seen, though it may be believed. Thus, the church prays in the liturgy of Evening Prayer: "Lord God, you have called your servants to ventures of which we cannot see the ending, by paths as yet untrodden, through perils unknown. Give us faith to go out with good courage, not knowing where we go, but only that your hand is leading us and your love supporting us."[23]

This way of thinking captures some of what Aristotle described as our "composite nature." It acknowledges our finitude. We are bodies for whom, even when all goes well, life moves inexorably through its course, ending in decline. But we are also free spirits, the truth of whose being cannot be entirely captured by describing the natural course or progression of an organism's life.

Most of the puzzles we encounter when we think about aging, or how best to think about aging, or how to age well, are a result of our two-sided being. On the one hand, we move inexorably through life toward old age and death. On the other hand, we quite naturally — and it seems rightly — long for more time, more life. On the one hand, we act virtuously when we display patience and humility in the face of life's limits. On the other hand, we quite naturally — and it seems rightly — strive to discover ways to retard aging and prolong life's banquet. On the one hand, we wear down and lose the zest and

23. *Lutheran Book of Worship* (Minneapolis: Augsburg Publishing House, 1978), p. 153.

freshness with which we once greeted each new day. On the other hand, we quite naturally — and it seems rightly — look for ways to regenerate our energies and revive our spirits.

We pass through the several stages of life in their fixed course, but we are also embarked on a journey of which we cannot see the ending. We have to ask, therefore, whether it might be a mistake to look for some way to think of our life as complete, all its threads gathered up into an integrated whole. We might say, as "Lead, Kindly Light," Newman's well-known hymn puts it, "Keep Thou my feet; I do not ask to see / The distant scene; one step enough for me."[24]

The philosopher Margaret Urban Walker has also tried to retain a sense of wholeness that is not dependent on any fixed course of stages or on the concept of a career. This sort of life — based on what she calls "lateral" rather than progressive integration — requires "no eventually unfulfillable demand for achievement or progress" through a series of stages to a satisfying end. Lateral integration focuses, she says, on "central lessons, tasks, pleasures, experiences, or bonds" that are important to us at different moments along the way, though they may not be linked together purposefully on some linear path or within a chronological narrative.[25] They are merely stopping points along the way, places we visit and then move on — not moments in a story held together by authorial purpose.

That is, I guess, one way to think about the journey of life, and it is not without its appeal. Perhaps it can give us a picture of a complete, flourishing life. But I cannot myself escape the sense that it leaves us, in the end, with lives more futile than flourishing. Embarked on the journey of life, we find many pleasant stopping places along the way. But these bear no necessary relation to each other, apart from the fact that we stop there, so our lives have continuity only in the obvious sense that "our physical trajectories are continuous."[26] It

24. http://www.hymns.me.uk/lead-kindly-light-favorite-hymn.htm. Accessed November 9, 2011.
25. Walker, "Getting Out of Line," p. 108.
26. Walker, "Getting Out of Line," p. 108.

is less a journey than a wandering — more Jean-Jacques Rousseau than Augustine. Barth's depiction, frankly religious, of life's journey may well be better; but, of course, it asks that we give up the attempt to see our lives as complete, integrated, and whole.

⧗   ⧗   ⧗

Where does this leave us? Perhaps in different places — some of us with Aristotle, others with Barth. Or, if it does not seem too quirky, I might say that it leaves us with a choice between John Hall Wheelock and Pope Benedict XVI.

Think back to "An Ancient Story," Wheelock's poem with which I began this chapter. The poet hears that young thrush singing from a hidden bough in the west wood nearby. The song reminds him of an earlier day when he and his beloved had stood there listening to that same song — and kissed in "the soft May-time green." Sing it again now, he says. Sing "That self-same song." Now as then, we are together still. Sing it again, and thereby bring back for us "That day when all was young."

But, of course, as the poet knows, "this may not be." A day will come when lover and beloved will be together still, but only in the sense that their bodies will be laid deep in the earth beside each other, under some "young springtime-flowering tree." Sing it again, the poet says. Sing your unchanged song then, too; for then as now we will be together still. Sing once more of "Life's fierce and tender glory / Once ours, when all was young."

This is the course of life. Then — now — then. We were once together — then — in this west wood listening to the thrush's song. We have grown older, but "now as then" we are together still, listening to that same song. A day will come when we are dead and buried, but "then as now" we will be together — deep within the earth, surrounded still by the thrush's unchanged song.

The poem gives us the course of a complete life. We are not embarked on a journey of which we cannot see the ending. On the contrary, we see it all too clearly. Deep in the earth our bodies shall be laid, for we are bodies — organisms — and this is what happens to organic life. Nature will carry on its inexorable course, and only the song of the thrush will remain. That is, indeed, a very ancient story.

And no one should say, it seems to me, that this story lacks power or beauty. It offers even a certain kind of satisfaction with the course life takes, an acceptance of our decline. If we want a picture of a complete life, I suspect we will not do much better.

But does this picture do justice to our composite nature — to the free spirit that indefinitely transcends the limits of our finite condition, that drove Aristotle to contrast the contemplative with the active life, that compelled Christians to think of themselves as embarked on a journey whose course they did not know? I think it does not; and I think, perhaps, the poem itself bears witness that it does not. The "pent-up fury and ardor" in the thrush's breast will not quite accept this course of life. It shatters the silence surrounding the lovers' graves "With love's high plaint amid things transitory." We might borrow a phrase from Reinhold Niebuhr and call that plaintive love song of the thrush "a tangent towards 'eternity' " in time.[27]

What is it that this plaintive love song desires? Is it only more time, an indefinite prolongation of the present "now" before the coming of the "then"? I suspect that could not satisfy lover and beloved, for they long for something qualitatively different — a love that never fades, that knows no "then" and "now" — of which their love can only be at best an image and intimation. Consider another poem by another minor romantic poet of the twentieth century, C. S. Lewis's "What the Bird Said Early in the Year."[28]

I heard in Addison's Walk a bird sing clear
"This year the summer will come true. This year. This year.

27. Reinhold Niebuhr, *The Nature and Destiny of Man,* vol. 2: *Human Destiny* (New York: Charles Scribner's Sons, 1964), p. 69.
28. C. S. Lewis, *Poems* (New York: Harcourt, Brace & World, Inc., 1964), p. 71.

"Winds will not strip the blossom from the apple trees
This year, nor want of rain destroy the peas.

"This year time's nature will no more defeat you,
Nor all the promised moments in their passing cheat you.

"This time they will not lead you round and back
To Autumn, one year older, by the well-worn track.

"This year, this year, as all these flowers foretell,
We shall escape the circle and undo the spell.

"Often deceived, yet open once again your heart,
Quick, quick, quick, quick! — the gates are drawn apart."

The gates of nature, though, always seem to slam shut again, and we are not quick enough to get through when they hint at possible escape from life's course. In his homily for the Easter Vigil in the year 2010, Pope Benedict XVI offered a different key to those gates. Noting how insistently human beings have sought a cure for death, a "medicine of immortality," he suggested that, even were we successful in that quest, "endless life would be no paradise." "The true cure for death," he said, "must be different. It cannot lead simply to an indefinite prolongation of this current life. It would have to transform our lives from within. It would need to create a new life within us, truly fit for eternity."[29] If Benedict is right, then until we taste that true cure in a medicine of immortality not of our own making, life can only remain — and must and should remain — incomplete, its threads not yet gathered up into any unified whole.

This, then, is our choice: "An Ancient Story." Or an Easter homily.

---

29. Benedict XVI, "Baptism as the Beginning of a Process: Easter Vigil Homily," *Origins* 39, no. 44 (April 15, 2010): 711-12.

Afterword

Thomas saw that a being obviously directed toward something else "cannot possibly have as his ultimate goal the preservation of his own existence!" In other words, the allaying of the thirst cannot consist simply in the mere continued existence of the thirster.

Josef Pieper, *Happiness and Contemplation*

His last Christmas letter contained a line that should be engraved above every geriatric door. He says that when asked if he feels like an old man he replies that he does not, he feels like a young man with something the matter with him.

Wallace Stegner, *The Spectator Bird*

HOW, THEN, SHALL we think about the related projects of age-retardation and life-prolongation? I imagine a conversation among three friends — Artie, Augie, and Frank — who have read the preceding six chapters. None of the friends supposes he has all the answers. Each is intrigued by the views of the other two. But each surely thinks his own view best captures how we ought to think. It might go something like this:

Frank: *I'm a little baffled by you two. Both of you say that you think life is a great good for human beings. You, Augie, even talk of it often as a blessing. But when I say we should try to prolong it as much as possible, neither one of you seems to agree. If life is so good, what's wrong with wanting more of it?*

Artie: *Of course, it's not wrong in every instance to want to prolong life. But have I ever really said to you that life itself, just more moments of it, is good? If I have, I should take it back. What's good is not simply more life but a complete life — a life that has a certain form and trajectory, that moves through stages that give it meaning. To die prematurely is to die before that trajectory is completed. But to want to hang on indefinitely after we've worked our way to the end of the story doesn't seem to me to get more of a good thing but, instead, to destroy what gives life its beauty.*

Frank: *Has it ever occurred to you that you might be too fond of the word "trajectory"?*

Artie: *Well, I'll try not to take refuge in it too often. But my point is simply that life isn't just a series of identical moments, coming one after the other and capable of indefinite extension. The moments of our lives have different meanings — and a different feel — precisely because they have different places in the whole. Surely you understand that. You wouldn't put the first paragraph of one of your essays at the end; its meaning depends on its location in the "trajec-*

tory" of the entire argument. For you more life is all that counts; for me a complete life is the good we should desire.

Frank: *I can't see that your notion of completion is more attractive than living on indefinitely at the peak of my powers, even if that means one moment is pretty much like those that come before and follow after it. They'd be good moments. More life sounds just fine to me.*

Artie: *Of course, you assume it would be at the peak of your powers. Do you know the story of Tithonus?*

Frank: *Yes, I know it and I've thought about it. I never said that prolonged aging was a desirable outcome of extending life. Longer life has to come in tandem with retarding aging in all possible ways, physical and mental. But why be a skeptic about what researchers may be able to accomplish? It's a brave man who bets against scientific progress.*

Artie: *I don't bet against it. I'm just not sure I'm ready to agree with you about what would constitute progress. Augie, you've been awfully quiet. Where do you come down on this question?*

Augie: *Well, I'm afraid that I agree with you both — and disagree with you both. I surely do agree with Frank that this life, even with its (sometimes very great) dangers and problems, is a blessing. So wanting more of it doesn't seem silly at all. But I also agree with you, Artie, that life seems to need what — avoiding the word "trajectory" — I'll just call a shape. And one of the things that gives it shape is that at some point it comes to completion.*

Frank: *So you agree with both of us. I'm not sure how that helps, but what about the disagreement? You said you also disagree with us.*

Augie*: Whether our ideal is simply more life or a complete life, in*

*either case something would still — it seems to me — be missing.
I think of us as being on the way toward something we can't quite
seem to get hold of. There's a thirst in us that isn't just a desire
for more life or just a desire for a complete life. I always think of
our lives in relation to God. So in one way it makes no difference
whether our lives are long or short; every moment in them is equidistant from God. In another way, of course, it does make a difference, since this life has a God-given shape that brings it to a kind of
earthly completion. That much Artie has right. But ours is a composite nature — we're organisms, but organisms who are drawn out of
ourselves toward God — and Artie sometimes sees only one part of
that picture. You, Frank, also see a part of the truth. It must be true
that we should often use our freedom to make life better, but if that
freedom to make and remake ourselves without limit were the only
truth about us, we'd be thinking of ourselves almost as gods, rather
than seeing ourselves as creatures in relation to God.*

Artie: *I'm not sure that's quite fair. I grant that we have what you
call a composite nature, that we're not just bodies. I just don't
know where all this talk about God comes from. Why don't we try
a slightly different angle? Part of a complete life is that we produce
those who will come after us and, having produced them, we must
eventually give way to them. So, even if it seems paradoxical, part
of flourishing as the creatures we are involves going to seed and,
eventually, dying.*

Augie: *You're right, I think, that producing and nurturing the next
generation, accepting that they will take our place, makes us better
people. It teaches us gratitude for the gift of our own lives.*

Frank: *Gratitude to whom?*

Augie: *I suppose that's a question Artie and I will have to take up
another time.*

Frank: *I can't say that I feel any strong urge to produce my replacement. I'm quite content to hang onto my life for as long as I can.*

Augie: *I didn't say you could be replaced; I said others would take your place. There's a difference.*

Artie: *You know, Frank, I'm not sure I believe that you would be content just to hang onto your own life indefinitely. It's natural to want to have children, to care for them, and to hand on to them our culture and beliefs. Not wanting to be replaced strikes me as narcissistic, not virtuous. In fact, in your quite different ways both you and Augie seem to forget that living on and on almost forever might become rather boring. We're bodies, after all. Human beings have limited capacities, and we'd eventually run out of new sources for enjoyment. The goodness of anything, even the best of things, eventually loses its power to delight.*

Augie: *Anything? What about the face of someone you love? Doesn't it at least suggest to you that there must be a face you would be content to love forever?*

Frank: *"Natural," as someone once said, is a word to conjure with. What's natural, it seems to me, is to exercise our rational freedom (call it "God-given freedom," if you like, Augie) in order to make our lives better and satisfy our desires more fully. Artie, you think we'll get bored if we live too long, because the capacities of human beings are limited. But let your imagination soar a bit. Already we're learning to take baby steps to enhance and reshape our lives. We're not bodies; we're free spirits who for now have to use organic bodies as the best prosthesis available. Someday we'll cast them off and be free of the limits you seem to like so much. And we'll get a real immortality, not the sort that Augie tries so hard to sell.*

Artie: *Those are fine words, Frank, though perhaps tinged with* *just a hint of desperation. But I don't think you can actually live in accord with your theory. I don't think you can love others, share a life with them and be fully involved in their lives, while all the time thinking of yourself as detached from the body that connects you to them. And there's something wrong with a theory that can't be lived.*

Augie*: And I marvel, Frank, that you find my talk of a resurrected body to be an unbelievable flight of fancy! What you can't tolerate, I'm afraid, is some contingency and mystery in life. But it's just that contingency that makes life sweet and, at the same time, suggests the promise of something more.*

⌧   ⌧   ⌧

Clearly, this is a conversation that could continue indefinitely; it need not come to an end here. Books, however, must end, and there is nothing particularly virtuous about forgetting that. We can never adequately summarize a conversation, but we can try to order our thinking.

The six preceding chapters have explored in different ways three general angles of vision that compete for our allegiance. Not all are equally persuasive or wise, at least in my view. But each makes central an aspect of our nature that is genuinely important, and, hence, each has a place in the conversation.

We may focus on the fact that human beings are organisms, embedded in the finite, natural world and following the trajectory of all organic life through relatively fixed stages of life — from modest beginnings, to full blossoming of capacities (including the capacity to generate a successor generation), and eventually "going to seed." From this first perspective, our commitment to age-retardation brings not only benefits but also harms, and should, in any case, be a modest commitment.

We may, by contrast, focus on that which distinguishes human beings from other organisms; namely, the freedom and reason that allow us indefinitely to transcend the limits of our finite condition, to make and remake ourselves in ever new ways that may promise (or threaten) to transcend our organic beginnings. From this second perspective, the projects of age-retardation and life-prolongation testify to what is most human about us — a freedom that knows few limits.

A third alternative discerns in us not only a nature marked by organic limits and rational freedom but also one that we may describe as "ecstatic." That is, we are characterized by a thirst that can be quenched neither by making our peace with the beauty and pathos of the limits of organic life nor by continual progress in the improvement and extension of our lives. We are, on this view, drawn out of ourselves toward God, and satisfaction of that longing could not possibly come from more of this life, however long extended. From this third perspective, we can and should think it a blessing that our lives are of limited duration — not because this life is not good, but because it cannot finally bring the completion needed for us truly to flourish.

My own view, like Augie's, is that the third perspective best captures the truth of who we are and who we are yet to become. There is sometimes good reason, as we age, to feel that something is the matter with us. There is also good reason to feel that we are young — with the youthfulness of eternity.

Index